CIVILITY

$16.95

CIVILITY

How It Fosters
Better Communities

Godfrey Harris

FIRST EDITION
1st Printing—August 2003

The Americas Group
9200 Sunset Blvd., Suite 404
Los Angeles, California 90069-3506
U.S.A.

☎	+ (1) 310 278 8038
FX	+ (1) 310 271 3649
EM	hrmg@aol.com
WWW	AMERICASGROUP.COM

ISBN:
0-935047-44-1

Library of Congress Cataloging-in-Publication Data

Harris, Godfrey, 1937-
  Civility : how it fosters better communities / Godfrey Harris.-- 1st ed.
      p. cm.
Includes bibliographical references and index.
  ISBN 0-935047-44-1
  1. Courtesy. 2. Etiquette. I. Title.
  BJ1533.C9H37 2003
  177'.1--dc21   2003009679

Printed in the United States of America by
Fidlar Doubleday, Kalamazoo, Michigan 49009

TABLE OF CONTENTS

DEDICATED TO

EDMUND F. LINDOP

—a teacher who understood that
the education of his students
involved more than just books,
assignments, and tests.

He wanted kids to have a strong
grounding in understanding how
our society had reached the point
in its journey where they would
take over its guidance.

But education for Ed Lindop was
also beyond the processing of basic facts
or providing a fresh analysis of the impact of
those facts. He believed that education
encompasses learning how to deal with
the challenges and opportunities
of everyday life as individuals
participating in a community.

If the educational process did not
yield practical results in the real world,
he felt he had failed in his effort
to bring his students to the point
of doing the job they
were meant to do in this world.

OTHER BOOKS BY GODFREY HARRIS

Corruption
The Essential Moving Planning Kit (with Mike Sarbakhsh)
The Essential Travel Planning Kit—1st and 2nd Editions
Grandparenting
The Essential Event Planning Kit—1st, 2nd, 3rd, and 4th Editions
Watch It!
Concentration—1st & 2nd Editions (with Kennith L Harris)
Let Your Fingers Do the Talking
Talk Is Easy
The Ultimate Black Book—3rd Edition
  (with Kennith L Harris & Mark B Harris)
Don't Take Our Word for It
How to Generate Word of Mouth Advertising
  (with Gregrey J Harris)
Promoting International Tourism—1st & 2nd Editions
  (with Kenneth M. Katz)
European Union Almanac—1st & 2nd Editions
  (with Hans J. Groll & Adelheid Hasenknopf)
The Panamanian Problem (with Guillermo de St. Malo A.)
Mapping Russia and Its Neighbors (with Sergei A. Diakonov)
Power Buying (with Gregrey J Harris)
Talk Is Cheap (with Gregrey J Harris)
The Fascination of Ivory
Invasion (with David S. Behar)
The Ultimate Black Book—2nd Edition (with Kennith L Harris)
The Ultimate Black Book—1st Edition
The Panamanian Perspective
Commercial Translations (with Charles Sonabend)
From Trash to Treasure (with Barbara DeKovner-Mayer)
Panama's Position
The Quest for Foreign Affairs Officers (with Francis Fielder)
The History of Sandy Hook, New Jersey
Outline of Social Sciences
Outline of Western Civilization

INTRODUCTION

This is the third in a trilogy of books I have written dealing with the general topic of how to make better communities for the future. As a lifelong student of political events, I started seeing the problems of communities growing and becoming less and less manageable. The three books emerged as my research deepened and my thinking matured. The issue that absorbed most of my concentration concerned why selfishness in the United States has apparently been on the increase over the past 50 years and how the citizens of communities in the 21st century might ameliorate the punishment it inflicts on society.

I see the turning point in social attitudes in the United States occurring in reaction to the feelings of profound loss at the assassinations of Jack Kennedy, Martin Luther King, and Bobby Kennedy, followed by a feeling of hopelessness in finding an acceptable solution to the morass of the Vietnam War, and capped off by the politically destructive revelations of the Watergate scandal—three major wounds to the American body politic within a period of 10 years. Trust evaporated, authority was questioned, drugs proliferated, and social patterns were challenged. And since the United States tends to lead the world in popular culture, it influenced attitudes in the rest of the world as well.

From the mid-1970s on, things did not get better through one presidential administration after another. Enter Bill Clinton. His presidency came to an end with a hesitant foreign policy, the collapse of the dot-com world, the flameout of the stock market, and his impeachment by the House, trial in the Senate, and punishment by a federal court for lying about matters related to the Monica Lewinsky affair. All of these examples of conduct over a period of nearly 50 years confounded the work of many religious, educational, and community leaders trying to return respect for the institutions society depends on to operate safely and comfortably in a complex world.

As a result of what was happening around us, I undertook the first book in this series, called *Grandparenting.* At its core, I suggested that if this knowledgeable, experienced, and available generation took on the conscious responsibility of showing its grandkids how to act and react to situations in public, we could begin to repair the damage and have much more enjoyable communities in which to live.

In the course of researching and writing *Grandparenting,* I became aware of the dozens of clearly corrupt acts that society condoned. It soon became evident that corruption permeated nearly every activity we need to sustain better communities. This corruption was not just the illegal variety, such as bribery and embezzlement, but also a host of other forms of cheating and unfairness that were sucking the will out of people to do what they knew was right. So I undertook the preparation of *Corruption* as a way of looking for a better means to overcome its negative effects than more guards, more laws, and more auditors. They clearly weren't very effective. It also occurred to me that given the pervasiveness of corruption throughout society, a solution wouldn't come from any politician, educator, or religious leader either. If society were going to deal with corruption seriously, it had to come from each of us doing our own part to make better communities for all.

This book, then, is about how to achieve that goal. Amazingly, it was not difficult to find acts of civility occurring all around us. By the same token, however, it was not hard to find even more examples of uncivil situations that need resolution.

Before going further, we need to understand our concept of civil behavior in a modern urban society. To us, civility is acting respectfully toward everyone and everything around us. It is exemplified by a common courtesy shown toward complete strangers in a public setting—holding a door for someone passing through, pulling over to allow another car to pass, speaking quietly to honor someone else's privacy. Civility is also evidenced when fulfilling the public responsibilities that others expect of us. These include helping the community when need arises, respecting the desires of others, obeying the law, and the like.

Two preliminary notes: I purposefully did not review the available literature on civility in history, political science, or sociology. I wanted to take a fresh look at the subject as it exists *now* to get a sense of what is actually before us. As a result, I have used very contemporary events to illustrate my points. Second, all quotations from non-American sources are included with their original spellings and syntax on the grounds that it is both more accurate as well as more respectful of how others use our common language.

It turns out that acting civilly is neither difficult nor complicated, but everyone reading these words realizes how often simple standards are breached in today's world. Bad manners, bad language, common discourtesies, uncivilized behaviors abound. All of us can remember the last time another driver reacted to something we did, either on purpose or by accident, by leaning on his horn, shouting something unintelligible, or gesturing rudely. All of us know the last time we were bothered by having to listen to a very personal conversation on a cell phone. All of us can recount the last time someone surged in front of us to get a better place in line or the last serving of a particular dish at a buffet table.

We hold that every gouge inflicted into the layers of civility protecting our communities represents a blemish on a better future. This book offers some ideas on how we might improve. I hope you will consider my suggestions and let me know what you think.

June 2003   *Godfrey Harris*

UNDERSTANDING CIVILITY

UNDERSTANDING CIVILITY

Civility in a society arises from the cumulative process of people acting in public in a helpful and considerate manner toward others. For example, civility is …

> … taking time to determine whether something occurring in public is making someone else uncomfortable or angry—and then taking steps to help rectify the situation.

> … participating in the political life of the community whether as an elected official, jury member, voter, active volunteer, or concerned citizen cognizant of current issues.

> … finding something of value and turning it over to authorities without hope of reward or recognition for the kindness.

> … offering to help someone down a step, across a road, through a gap, out a door, or up a path

without requiring a particular request or regard for one's own needs at that moment.

Civility assumes that society will reap positive benefits when its members behave in appropriate ways toward others. But civility is having a tough time these days. A survey taken in 2002 by the Gallup Organization concluded that Americans are whining more and tolerating less personal inconvenience than ever before. Their sense of community and concern for others seem to be diminishing.

We believe that when people consistently act helpfully and considerately toward other members of society—without hope of specific reward—they tend to feel good about themselves and the community becomes a better place for it. Better communities add up to a better country and then hopefully a better world.

Civility, in our view, is the Golden Rule extended beyond the boundaries of family and friends. Every major religion embraces its tenets. In Christian tradition, it is usually stated:

***Do unto others
as you would have them do unto you.****

The Koranic version of the Golden Rule^ was summed up in the following way for us by the principal English

CIVILITY

---

* The sources for most of the statements in quotation marks or indented in italics can be found under the appropriate page number in the Bibliographic Notes section of the Appendix. The exceptions are those quotations fully identified in the text, quotations from my own writings, or when quotation marks are used to highlight sarcasm. A caret mark—^— such as used above indicates that an additional comment or further information on this particular point can be found in the Bibliographic Notes section.

translator for Turkish philosopher and author Harun Yahya:

Be forgiving to others
as you would love God to be forgiving to you.

The Jewish version was recounted by Rabbi Hillel (whether the Elder or his son of the same name and title is not known), who wrote in the first century that all of God's teachings can be summed up in a single sentence:

Whatever is hateful unto thee,
do it not unto thy fellow.

Rabbi Hillel went on to note: "This is the whole law; the rest is but commentary." Hillel's version when re-stated positively can be seen to mean: Concern for the well-being of others is of equal importance to one's own well-being in the same time and place.

Yet this book arises precisely because of the gulf that has developed between Hillel's belief and the attitudes and activities displayed by so many people in public. In fact, it is probable that most of us have experienced more acts of *incivility* than have witnessed the kind of civil behavior described earlier.

- Take the issue of cell phones. Their use has certainly added to a more civil lifestyle for many and has just as certainly led to a degree of incivility for others. Being able to connect with emergency personnel after an accident is just one example of the former; endangering someone else while driving and using a cell phone is an example of the latter. As one of our friends complained to an elected official: "Left-handed drivers tend to hold cell phones in their left hands and to their left ears. Their right hand [is] on the steering wheel, [making] it impossible to operate the [left side] controls such as turn signals at the same time."

- Take the case of the Ivory Coast in Africa: *The New York Times* notes that "what began ... as a struggle for the rights of disenfranchised ethnic groups [has descended] into lawlessness, gangsterism, and a series of unspeakable atrocities." Civilization, corrupted by money and power, is disintegrating in what was a very civilized country. Now "guns are as plentiful as mangoes in March."

- Still another example of extraordinary incivility emerged recently in Nigeria, where two normally peaceful local tribes—the minority fishermen of the Ijaw and the majority farmers of the Itsekiri— caused the shutdown of Nigeria's oil exports in a fierce, armed struggle over who would control the local government and the millions of dollars for patronage generated by the income from oil. As a retired Itsekiri judge noted: "Maybe if there had been no oil, these tensions would not have been created." In other words, the civilizing benefits of oil for some had become the engine of incivility for others.

- In the small Indian town of Ayodhya, archaeology, religion, and politics have mixed with horrific results. In 1992, a Hindu mob demolished a 16th century mosque they claimed was built atop an earlier Hindu temple marking the birthplace of Rama, Hinduism's supreme deity. The Hindus want to build a new temple on the site; the Muslims say there is no proof a temple was ever there. The attack set off nationwide religious riots that left more than 2,000 people dead.^ Given the bad blood and depth of feelings on both sides of this issue, new facts are unlikely to dissolve any of the religious emotions that have caused the level of incivility experienced to date.

Although in no way related, a successful democracy is dependent on some of the same attributes that also contribute to a community's level of civility. For example, democracies and civil societies both depend on:

> *Voluntary association[s], a tolerance for nonconformism and pluralism, a shared belief in the dignity of the individual, an autonomous sphere of economic activity, separation of political power from religious authority and a belief in the legitimacy of dissent.* *

All of these attributes tend to be difficult to achieve when a society lacks experience in meeting its challenges. Each society, anxious for the benefits of democracy, has to learn how to cope with these conflicting values.

As a result, if achieving civility were as easy as passing a law or buying peaceful conditions in areas where law-

---

* Reminder: References for this and other quotations are found in the Bibliographic Notes section of the Appendix under the appropriate page number.

lessness abounds, the United States would have long ago adopted such procedures. But bushels of new laws in America regulating all kinds of behaviors as well as billions of dollars in welfare payments for those suffering from poverty and other deprivations have proven incapable of resolving the problems in civility that the U.S. is suffering.

Remember that civility, in the context of this book, looks to activities undertaken and courtesies rendered in *public* settings. While manners and attitudes exhibited toward relatives and friends have purposefully been put beyond the scope of this book, etiquette, courtesy, and respect are not totally divorced from what is discussed here. The teachings and values learned in a family setting almost naturally carry over to behavior toward others in a public arena. So the more courtesy and respect demanded at home—whether by parents, siblings, grandparents, or others—the better off society becomes.^

We hold strongly to the belief that *situations* dictate how people behave in public settings as a result of external stimuli. We also believe that those situations should not affect how people react toward *others* in those same settings. For example:

- Noise, physical movement, and all manner of verbal comments are part of a baseball game or an evangelical revival but would be discouraged by a librarian in a reading room and not tolerated by police trying to control a mob.

- By the same token, courtesy, respect, and concern for others are not altered by whether a person is in a box seat at a stadium, at a political rally in an arena, or at a carrel in the stacks. The teachings of mom and dad or the examples set by brother or sister on how one treats others on a personal level remain the same whatever the setting.

At the core of every civil society is *trust*—a condition that allows individuals to rely on others, particularly complete strangers, to operate within a set of generally accepted rules and to deal with each other in a reasonably truthful and honorable manner. As a result, everyone is rightfully worried about the recent deterioration of trust in political, religious, business, charitable, and sports organizations in this country as the amount of corruption has exploded.^ So much distrust and dishonesty seem to exist in so many areas of our culture that both have become of genuine concern to a number of institutions beyond law enforcement.

At the New York Stock Exchange, for instance, seven specialist firms are responsible for making orderly markets in the thousands of issues traded on a daily basis for hundreds of billions of dollars. That means that these firms are expected to smooth out moment-to-moment external market conditions by buying or selling shares for their own accounts. By interfering from time to time with buy/sell demand, these firms can help stabilize a stock's price. It has now been revealed that some operatives in these firms have been buying and selling for their *own* accounts just in advance of executing some large trade for an institutional investor. The practice is called "front-running" and has been made possible by the recent change in pricing shares from increments of eighths of a dollar to one penny. Since these specialists determine the actual price at which any trade will occur, they can create a locked-in profit for themselves—by raising or lowering the price of a share to an outside buyer by a penny or two over what *they* had just paid or sold the same stock for. Front-running has created a major crisis in trust among millions of investors.^

Another example: One of the Big Five accounting firms has confronted the issue of trust and honesty directly. It is trying to regain public acceptance of accounting processes after Arthur Andersen & Co. helped Enron to doctor its books to the detriment of individual investors. Perhaps you have seen the television ad that has been produced for PricewaterhouseCoopers to address the problem.

The ad shows a fancy new sedan parked cheek by jowl with an older-model car in a deserted parking garage. The cars are so close to each other that the owner of the new car has no hope of getting in on the driver's side. As a result you see him laboriously clambering through the passenger side, over the center console, then wedging himself behind the wheel. Finally there, he smiles, takes a deep breath, starts the engine, and pulls away. But in the struggle to get in, he has completely forgotten how close he is to the car at his side. Instantly, you hear the telltale sound of crunching metal and shattered glass as the sedan's sideview mirror clips the same accessory of the car next to him.

The driver continues forward for a little distance, a look of resignation on his face. With a slight shrug of the shoulders, he is clearly considering leaving, thinking that it serves the other guy right for parking so close. But moments later the car stops, the screen goes to black, and the following simple statement appears in white:

The softest pillow is a clear conscience.

The final scene in the ad shows the driver of the sedan stopping, getting out of his car, and placing his business card under the windshield wiper of the damaged vehicle.

If reinforcing the tenets of honesty requires a national television ad, the entire issue of morality in our society also seems in need of some repair. Look at the statistics circulating on the Internet of transgressions committed by the 535 members of the 107th U.S. Congress:

29	Accused of spousal abuse
7	Arrested for fraud
8	Arrested for shoplifting
19	Accused of kiting checks
3	Did time for assault
84	Drunk-driving arrests
117	Filed for bankruptcies _two_ or more times

Given the deterioration of trust in our society, why can't we just clear up the underlying causes with a few trials, some big fines, and a dose of stern sermons from the nation's pulpits to put the country back on a civil course? It's not so easy. Here is a short list of the reasons why.

- _Crowded conditions._ When people are packed into urban settings, when they are pushed around because of these conditions by strangers, people become impatient and impatience fosters cheating on the rules to overcome the impediments hindering the way forward.

- *Too many pressures.* When we have assigned ourselves too many tasks in too short a period of time, we tend to cut corners to meet our obligations. Cutting corners usually results in some form of incivility to others.

- *Questionable values.* When people believe it is important to earn a lot of money for the sake of achieving prominence on the "leader board" of success or show others where they shop, where they vacation, where they work, and what clubs they belong to, incivility results from overreaching in trying to achieve these kinds of goals.

- *Fundamental disagreements.* When people reduce the views of others to disparaging categories, shorthand labels, or name calling, it becomes an easy way to avoid the hard work of understanding another's point of view. As columnist Nicholas Kristof notes: "[T]he war [in Iraq] has pulverized the civility of discourse. Each side assumes the other is not just imbecilic but also immoral, when in truth … each side is genuinely highminded: one is driven by the horror of war and the other by horror of Saddam [Hussein]."

- *Other concerns.* When people are involved in a struggle against the effects of poverty or the unfairness of injustice—or are focused on attaining a singular goal—they seem to have no energy or mind for what constitutes civil behavior.

From another perspective, someone might ask how the attributes of civility can be promoted. One answer is to evaluate constantly the need to change the boundaries on what a civil society needs. In England, for example, British Sign Language (BSL) has recently been recognized as an official language along with Gaelic and Welsh. Although the language serves the needs of a tiny fraction of the population—barely 70,000 Britons out of a population of nearly 60 million—BSL will now have the same status as spoken English for school graduation, college entrance, and other communication needs. In Vail, Colorado, bottom land is so scarce and valuable that the ski resort refuses to sanction space for a cemetery. Instead, the Town Council is considering a memorial park where inscriptions, plaques, and benches could be inscribed in memory of the dead and where urns for ashes could be kept. "These days it is not … about … remains, [but] about being memorialized."

Another answer is to recognize the different ways in which civility can be promoted. Daniel Patrick Moynihan, the late U.S. senator from New York, early in his public career was asked to research the Labor Department's office needs. His report famously noted that federal buildings "must provide visual testimony to the dignity, enterprise, vigor, and stability of the American government." In other words, the amount of space and its utility—pure economics—should not be the only issue when the full extent of society's interests are taken into consideration.

Maintaining some aspects of civility, once their purpose is recognized and accepted, may be achieved by enforceable rules. In London, for example, taxi drivers must agree to keep their cabs clean as a condition of being issued a license. While this is a matter of pride for most drivers working in a rainy climate, empowering the police to issue citations for dirty cabs ensures nearly total compliance

When law is not required to maintain civility, it can often be supported by ritual. Children are hammered until they learn to say in their language "please," "thank you," and "excuse me." In court, opposing counsels are required to address the judge rather than each other. By taking the individuals out of every confrontation, anger is lowered and reasonable discourse can proceed. In the House of Representatives of the United States, members are required to address any direct questions or comments about another member to the chair; thus even the most withering criticism or scathing attacks seem directed at the speaker. In parliamentary debate in England, every hostile questioner is still answered with a reference to "My Honorable Friend."^

These are little touches, for sure, but nevertheless useful ways of diffusing the passions of the moment and preserving the rules and behavior patterns that bind a society together. In fact, when you look closely at achieving civility in public settings, you find it is the little touches that count much more than any grand gesture such as teaching the topic in schools, conducting off-site trainings for corporate leaders, or enduring lectures from religious leaders.

Laughter also has to be one of the great tonics for protecting society from the potential for incivility. The ability to laugh at the mysteries and mistakes of life has a wonderful tendency to reduce tensions. Take the serious topic of war with Iraq in the winter of 2003:

- TV host David Letterman: "France said this week they need more evidence to convince them Saddam is a threat. Yeah, the last time France asked for more evidence it came rolling through Paris with a German flag on it."

- In a similar tone and at the same time, a U.S. senator offered the following question and answer: "How many Frenchmen does it take to defend Paris?" "I don't know. It's never been tried."

At its heart, though, civilization is about *respect* for others. Even those civilizations that pride themselves on unbridled individual freedoms know that one person's freedom does not include the right to infringe on someone else's independence of thought, movement, or action. In short, respecting the other person's interests, rights, and positions at all times must be uppermost in people's minds. If another person's interests, rights, and positions are respected, it is likely that the individuals in that community will live in peace and harmony with each other. It is one of those simple statements like the Golden Rule—easy to express, hard to achieve.

- Look at the example of graffiti, the selfish statement of certain individuals about their skills, power, or bravery. While a few have argued that graffiti is an art form for those who cannot afford to express their feelings on more conventional media, most hold that it is a profound sign of disrespect for the larger public whose property is defaced by unwanted tags, signs, and words.

- Take the example of the rules of the road, one of the areas of modern society where the tension between civil and bad behavior is always on edge. Recent studies have shown that about 7 percent of all road trips in the United States are made on foot. Nearly all the other 93 percent are in motor vehicles. When traffic engineers worry exclusively about moving the 93 percent in the most efficient and convenient fashion possible—their usual posture—they tend to ignore the safety and well-being of the 7 percent who are walking. If society fails to see the needs of the 7 percent by pouring praise and promotions on the bureaucrats who serve drivers, only disharmony and distrust occur. If the 7 percent see the actions of drivers and their bureaucratic supporters as selfish and inconsiderate, they may do things that confound the rights of the majority. When the seeds of incivility of one group toward another sprout and grow, they can become very difficult to uproot.

- There is a passionate group of activists who believe vehemently that trade in ivory products harms the well-being of elephant herds in Africa. A much smaller and considerably less demonstrative group of conservationists, ivory collectors, and animal-care specialists argue differently. They are influenced by the destruction wild elephants can inflict on modern human settlements, the lack of sufficient space and money in national parks to care for protected herds, and the value of ivory harvested from dead elephants for artistic, decorative, and practical purposes. The debate over how to set rules to protect the elephants while recognizing on-the-ground realities comes every four years as changes in the enforcement of a treaty—the Convention on International Trade in Endangered Species (CITES)—are negotiated. The contrast between the generally civil discussions inside the meeting halls and the animated demonstrations outside the convention arena is an example of what happens when respect suffers and rationality deserts reasonable people.

In each of these examples, the key for society is to look for ways to reconcile the competing interests—particularly those involving a single majority and multiple minorities.^ Finding fair and proportionate answers is not always easy; in most cases, people seem to give up long before an issue can be wisely resolved. Take the case of hot cross buns. Most British schools have now been forbidden to serve these warm sweet rolls with icing made in the shape of the cross—a traditional Easter treat. Local politicians said they were concerned that children of non-Christian faiths would be offended. It turned out to be an easy answer but not a satisfying solution. As one conservative MP noted: "Anything that comes from an ethnic minority is fine, while anything Christian is wrong." The Muslim Council of Britain called the decision "very, very bizarre. We are quite capable of articulating our own concerns....We do not need to rely on other people to do it for us."^

While the formula that provides balance without seeming to pander to the political correctness gods is difficult, finding it can avoid the kind of hatreds, enmities, and distrust so common to uncivil behavior. In thinking about the task of crafting reasonable compromises, forget about the big issues of race, abortion, education, and the like. They engender too much emotion at the present time. Think rather about something as ephemeral as the Oscars, Hollywood's annual effort to reward the best in film making of the previous year.

To some in the entertainment industry and related fields, the Oscars are of vital importance, a momentous event in their personal well-being. If you live in Los Angeles, you are inundated by the barrage of advertisements, dominated by media coverage of the numerous other award presentations, and as a result you come to think of the Academy Awards as crucial to life itself. Moviegoers, wherever they live, also take a passionate interest in who wins. But for the vast majority of people in the rest of the world, Oscar time is a moment of fluff and ostentation and perhaps a guide to determine which American movies to try to see in the ensuing months. On a scale of things that really matter, they are unimportant, "an essentially American phenomenon blown far out of proportion [by the media]." It is a lesson that we are often shortsighted in our attitudes.

To separate the real from the fantasy, then, is not always easy, but until we consistently and conscientiously become attuned to the interests, rights, and positions of those who have a different perspective in our communities, we will not enjoy a return to the civil society so many of us miss—a society in which peace and tranquility reign, where respectful behavior counts, and where the rights of everyone are honored. That is not to say that every demand of every minority must be accommodated in the way the minority wishes. On the contrary, civilization is about compromise and finding a means to accommodate one's own desires to the needs of others. And equally important, this is not about laws but about *understanding*. And significantly, it is not fixing things for an eternity but fixing them for the next few months or years until new circumstances dictate a review and further change.

Civilization, in other words, is not carved in stone but remains a dynamic, changing condition that demands our attention. We hope it gets yours as you continue reading this book.

CASE STUDIES
IN CIVILITY

CIVILITY

INTRODUCTION

Civility is not so much a set of rules or a series of do's and don'ts as it is a host of circumstances that handled in a balanced way can foster a society in which its inhabitants are trustful, respectful, and comfortable.^ It is not always easy. Take the recent opening of a freeway extension in Los Angeles. The resulting traffic noise has created "both mental and physical health hazards" for those who live nearby. Building sound walls, restricting trucks, lowering speed limits are all attempts at making a freeway work for everybody in a community.

This chapter looks at a number of different aspects of civility that if replicated elsewhere or emulated on a grander scale would likely make all of our communities better places in which to live. In reviewing these case studies, please note that nearly all acts of civility occur within the framework of one of the following categories of behavior:

Natural	These are the acts of civility that are automatic—responses borne of years of habit or teachings by parents, ministers, teachers, counselors, and other role models.
Obvious	These are acts that seem programmed into the human genome: what to do in the case of a burning building, a car accident, a lost child looking for a parent.
Difficult	These are the acts of civility that require some discomfort to perform: when help is needed by a single woman, a homeless man, a person who doesn't speak the language, a lost child.
Ambivalent	These are the acts of civility that you may not be qualified to perform: an injured person requiring a doctor, a dirty and perhaps incoherent beggar, someone in bodily danger that would put a savior in even more danger.

Individual response is then a function of not only knowing what to do but of one's own personality and capabilities. Clearly the civil thing to do when an individual sees a person appearing to drown is to plunge into the water to rescue him or her. But if the observer is unable to swim, he or she cannot be of much good in those circumstances. As a result, another form of response may be required to accomplish the same goal.

One further thought. Just as acts of civility fit within a specific framework of reactions that can make for a better society, so we hold that acts of *incivility* remaining unremarked, uncorrected, or unpunished give license to the perpetrators to commit further such acts and give rise to abetting others to show an equal amount of disrespect for the society by increasing their own selfish behavior.

With these thoughts in mind, please look at the case studies that follow.

SARS

Severe acute respiratory syndrome (SARS) first appeared on the world's health watch in mid-March 2003 when reports of a mysterious illness infecting and killing people in East Asia began to surface.^ While the disease had all the earmarks of a form of pneumonia—high fever, chills, headache, malaise, and body aches, along with a subsequent dry cough accompanied by breathing difficulties—it was also contagious. Other pneumonias are not. That worried health officials at the outset. This new disease was operating in a way that they had never encountered before.

At first it was thought that people were catching SARS by being in close contact with those suffering from it—family care givers and health professionals. But subsequent cases gave rise to the possibility that the virus was being transmitted by insects, rodents, surface contacts, and other indirect means. Early cases also indicated that the incubation period—the time before symptoms were felt or seen—varied; worse, the timing when a carrier of the disease was most infectious seemed to be inconsistent from country to country, case to case. As the mystery surrounding the disease deepened, some scientists began to suspect that they were dealing with different strains of the virus and/or even mutations.

Nevertheless, as soon as health authorities became aware of the new mystery illness, its cause, transmission, and treatment have been under intense scrutiny. International organizations and governmental authorities around the globe mobilized to track its spread as well as share information on the pathology and treatment of patients. Laboratories in many countries scrambled to try to identify the structure of the virus.^

In relatively short order, medical specialists found evidence to lead them to believe that the disease originated in China's Quangdong Province. A doctor there traveled to Hong Kong in February 2003 for a wedding, stayed on the ninth floor of the Metropole Hotel, and was visited by friends and relatives. These visitors, others who occupied the same floor, and wedding guests were infected by the virus and carried it back to their Hong Kong high-rise apartment buildings as well as to their homelands in Vietnam, Canada, Singapore, and elsewhere. A doctor who treated one of the early carriers unknowingly brought SARS to the U.K, and the U.S. A prominent World Health Organization (WHO) doctor who originally identified the disease as something new also eventually died after treating patients in Hanoi.

When microbiologists at the University of Hong Kong announced that "SARS is caused by a previously unknown member of the family of viruses known as coronavirus," health authorities were pleased. As soon as samples of the virus became available, others went to work on its DNA to determine what drugs might work and how a vaccine might be created. In the meantime, other laboratories came up with contradictory findings, leaving scientists even more puzzled. Despite the doubts and confusion about so many aspects of SARS, a whole range of measures went into effect to try to stop the spread of the disease:

CASE STUDIES

- In Hong Kong, many bus drivers and office workers started wearing protective masks regularly. But kids didn't like wearing them and taxi drivers refused to because they said it scared away fares. Businesspeople, meanwhile, struggled with the question of whether masks put their customers at ease or frightened them. Elsewhere, El Al ordered all flight staff to wear masks on Asian flights and made them available to passengers as well.

- In the United States, Asians noted that fear of SARS "struck them even harder than the Sept[ember] 11 [2001] attacks and the general economic malaise that followed." Their businesses have shrunk. Worldwide, economists estimated that SARS "could drain $10.6 billion" and as much as $16 billion from the 2003 GDP forecasts for countries in East Asia.^

- In Singapore, the government ordered mandatory quarantines for anyone suspected of carrying SARS and closed all schools from day-care centers to junior colleges. When new cases continued to arise, electronic wrist tags were ordered and closed-circuit television cameras installed to insure that the quarantine's strictures were obeyed. In addition and after the death of a priest who tended a SARS patient, the Roman Catholic Church eliminated individual confessions, handholding in church, and communion wafers being placed on the tongues of parishioners.

- Companies in the U.S. and elsewhere discouraged travel to China; business at the 2003 Canton Fair was said to be off 90% from a year ago. Continental Airlines, meanwhile, dropped flight after flight as passengers canceled trips to the Far East. Other airlines began more rigorous cleaning of aircraft after stops in countries with a high incidence of SARS.

- Airlines that continued to operate began screening passengers, looking for and asking about symptoms; airport medical facilities have been flooded with people seeking treatment after an intercontinental flight seated near someone who coughed or seemed ill. The Rolling Stones postponed a series of concerts booked for Hong Kong. The Chinese government ordered cancellation of a weeklong spring holiday that promised to have millions traveling all over the country. In addition, all of Beijing's movie theaters, billiard parlors, dance halls, karaoke clubs, Internet cafes, and even chess rooms were closed.

- As one infectious disease specialist said: "I don't think we know where we're going on this one; we're in the third or fourth line of a three-act play." A WHO official called the threat posed by SARS "unprecedented" and noted that "the virus has … demonstrated its explosive power."

Dealing with the sudden and virulent nature of something like SARS demonstrates the importance of government in the promotion of civility. In this case, people's very survival may depend on how a government reacts. The new Chinese leadership under Hu Jintao, after firing the health minister and mayor of Beijing, immediately allocated $360 million to fund new preventive measures. Nearly everyone in China feels the need to protect $50 billion in *new* annual foreign investment as well as the 2008 Summer Olympic Games.

At the most basic level, each of us is responsible in some way for the well-being of everyone else around us. Civilization also provides the organizational base to fight something that no individual can combat on his or her own. In the case of a disease like SARS, we can't see it, we are not sure how to protect ourselves from it, and there is literally no certain way to get away from it in a modern urban setting. The problem requires some kind of *organization* to bring together specialists as well as mechanisms to battle it. Clearly civilization provides the foundation for an institution like *government* to deal with problems faced in common. In the case of SARS, individuals must obey quarantine rules, must wash their hands, must safely dispose of face masks, must report symptoms so that anyone they have been in contact with can be isolated from others, and must do whatever else is asked of them.

SARS also shows the level of our interdependency. When we realize that civility can do good—protect us from the spread of illness, for example—and when we realize that we must take an active part in its workings to make it effective for everybody, we see the importance of the subject of this book.

LOOTING

The realization that governments count was made evident in the closing days of the Iraq War in April 2003. As the invading U.S. and U.K. forces gained military control of the major cities in the country, the civilian elements of the Iraqi government collapsed. When police functions evaporated, intense looting resulted. Whether out of past deprivations, anger, greed, sport, or other motives, the accepted rules of behavior in Iraqi society ceased to apply.

It seemed to start with a few people defying those rules to take whatever was available. Hundreds, then thousands followed. Whether they were acting out of rage against past actions of the Baath Party, bitterness at what Saddam Hussein's regime had brought upon them, or the poverty inflicted by years of United Nations--mandated sanctions, or simply taking advantage of an extraordinary opportunity to help themselves to goods they would never, themselves, be able to afford, their actions seemed to infect an entire population. It has happened before.

- When riots broke out in Los Angeles in 1992 in protest of the acquittal of police officers accused in the beating of an unruly individual named Rodney King, mobs formed and broke into dozens of stores in the midcity area to steal what they could and burn what they couldn't. Television cameras photographed the scenes from helicopter platforms high above the streets.

- In 1989, when the U.S. invaded Panama to arrest Gen. Manuel Noriega, looting began as soon as it was clear that the Panamanian Defense Force and its police functions had disintegrated. Without anyone to enforce the law, people climbed fences, crawled through windows, broke down doors, and smashed through every conceivable barrier to decimate retail establishments in the commercial districts. When the criminal elements in the mobs couldn't find enough of value left in the stores to satiate their greed, they turned on the residential neighborhoods to continue their marauding. At that point, the residents of these middle- and upper-class areas drew their weapons, drew a line around their homes, and drew on their friends to organize a no-holds-barred defense.^

- In Iraq, the looters did not seem to concentrate on commercial establishments. Instead, television pictures emphasized looters attacking government facilities, ripping the corrugated roofing off buildings, wheeling away the desk chairs of bureaucrats piled high with electronic gear. We saw kids carrying off computer monitors with their entrails of cords and keyboards trailing behind. One family was shown dragging a giant diesel generator behind a truck in a shower of sparks, another piling couches and tables into a pickup truck, and still another man seating himself behind the wheel of a government bus he intended to drive home. The newspapers reported how the national museum was stripped of priceless antiquities that were dug out of reinforced subterranean catacombs as well as ripped out of display cabinets. The devastation was less than originally estimated, but nonetheless, priceless items were lost, including the famous gold and ivory harp of Ur.

All of these examples prove that governments play an essential part in the maintenance of civil behavior. It matters not whether a government is controlled by democratic forces or by those with authoritarian tendencies. Without its presence, society is reduced to individuals, family units, and roving gangs all vying to satisfy whatever goal they have set for themselves. They have no regard for outsiders of their group. We may not always like what governments do, but we have to recognize that they provide the structure and the personnel that can mount a defense quickly and effectively against the unwanted behavior of elements of a society.

Governments also know that they can be overwhelmed by the actions of mobs; it has happened time and again in countless countries. Perhaps the most vivid recent scene captured on television occurred in Belgrade, Serbia, in 2000. A huge crowd had gathered at the parliament building and became so large and oppressive that the troops surrounding the building were simply overwhelmed by the sheer numbers they faced. Their commanders doubted whether the structure they were supposed to defend warranted the effort. As the mob entered the building like water finding a downhill path, so the military forces dissolved into the crowd, and Slobodan Milosevic's government came to an end.

This episode reminds us that governments acting to enforce civil behavior are not the last word; at some point they become only the agents of the general population. In the end—and at some point in the course of human events—governments must do what the people want them to do. It is the individual, then, who holds the ultimate power to enforce the rules and create a civil society.

CIVILITY

DISTRIBUTED INTELLIGENCE

Michael Crichton writes about the power of distributed intelligence in his book *Prey*.

> *Most people watching a flock of birds or a school of fish assumed there was a leader, and that all the other animals followed the leader. But birds and fish [have] no leaders. [They] respond to a few simple stimuli among themselves, and the result is coordinated behavior [called distributed intelligence.]*

> *[For example,] ... individual birds [are not] genetically programmed for flocking behavior. On the contrary, flocking simply emerged ... [from] rules like, "Stay close to the birds nearest you, but don't bump into them." [These] ... low-level rules [are] called emergent behavior ... behavior ... that was not programmed into any member of the group.*

> *But...emergent behavior [is] erratic. "Trying to program distributed intelligence is like telling a five-year-old to go to his room and change his clothes. He may do that, but he is equally likely [to become distracted, unpredictable and end up doing] something else."*

Civility seems to be a little like distributed intelligence. No one has programmed it or has the power to command individuals to behave in a specific way toward each other. Rather, civility has emerged from thousands of years of human experience with various types of group behavior. As ants swarm, termites mound, and bees dance, so humans exhibit behavior on their own that taken together can result in better communities.

But like the five-year-old in the excerpt from Crichton's story above, the society has to keep the individual focused on some common goals to achieve civility just as hunger focuses the lions in a pride to keep on stalking prey until they are successful in their quest.

CIVILITY

IT STARTS WITH HUMILITY

When things seem to be rolling—but you don't know why and you don't know how to sustain the trend—it turns out to be even more frustrating than when you do all the right things and don't get the results desired. It is a strange experience to be carried along by the fates rather than by your cleverness and hard work. It happened to our publisher with one of our books. The book began selling consistently in large quantities on the Internet, and we could not figure out what was driving the sales. Because the actual sales were being made by a third party, we had no opportunity to quiz buyers on how they had learned of *The Essential Event Planning Kit*.^ After a while, we became desperate to know whether price, title, subject matter, a review, word of mouth—what???—was working so well for us. But we have never actually found out. It was a very humbling experience.

It then dawned on us that civility *also* starts with humility. If you are humble about the effect you are able to create on the situation around you, it is very hard to do things that others would consider impolite or rude. On the other hand, if you have no clue about what is the basis for your success—or you are in the habit of fooling yourself—you can become arrogant and arrogance can breed *incivility*.

Take the case of the 20-something kids working for a Canadian real estate firm in Southern California. They were selling condominium conversions to frightened renters who thought that if they didn't agree to buy their apartments, there would be no place left for them to rent. The kids who signed up the renters all thought they were brilliant and that the Porches parked in the lot resulted from their hard work. Those of us who had been around the track a few times knew that these kids were riding a wave, a fashion, a trend that they had not started and could not control, and they would have no idea how or when it might end. But they took the credit, nevertheless, for the income they were generating, and the cars were proof of their success.

But as they became more and more arrogant in their dealings with prospective buyers, the buyers became more resistant to the pushing. Eventually, the market for condominium conversions cooled as interest rates rose and profits receded. The 20-something kids could not earn the commissions they had become used to drawing, and eventually they left. Many drifted back to graduate school, one hopes to learn how the real world works. Most of them, however, held on to their fancy cars.

The point is that we have noticed that people who are humble about what they can accomplish or what they are responsible for always tend to act in a civil way toward others; their civility is then reflected in how others conduct their own dealings.

THE LAWSUIT

In the United States, lawsuits have become the tool of choice for one group to try to enforce civil behavior on another individual or organization. The mantra seems to be

- Perceive a wrong, sue 'em.
- Experience a slight, sue 'em.
- Sustain an injury, sue 'em.
- Find a mistake, sue 'em.
- Discover a fraud, sue 'em.
- Suspect an error, sue 'em.

It doesn't matter whether there is sufficient evidence or whether the cause is just or not, lawsuits are the great American civic equalizer. In other days, people sought the help of clergy, royalty, the sheriff, a "godfather," or some other authority greater than themselves to enforce the rules. Now no one need go further than some cluck who has survived three years of a fly-by-night law school, passed the bar, and participated in a tort case or two to seek redress for whatever grievance is considered real or imaginary.^

In a modern democratic society is this an appropriate way to proceed? Probably. But it didn't come about through master planning. The economics of graduate school education are such that all a university need do to churn out new lawyers is reserve a few classrooms, add some extra tables and chairs, purchase a few specialized books, and hire some part-time teachers to expose students to the way the law has developed over the years. Contrast the cost of providing a legal education to the cost of maintaining a medical facility or providing scientific laboratories for other students and you see why universities have produced more lawyers and MBAs than radiologists and research chemists.

With so many hungry lawyers going into business, it was only a matter of time before they discovered the thicker veins of legal ore and how to extract their maximum value. The result is that not all lawsuits seeking redress for uncivil behavior are valid. Each year something called the Stella Awards—named for the 81-year-old Stella Liebeck, who successfully sued McDonald's for injury she sustained when she spilled hot coffee on herself—are given for the least meritorious lawsuits filed and won! Here is a just a sampling:

- Kathleen Robertson of Austin, Texas, was awarded $750,000 by a jury^ after breaking her ankle tripping over a toddler running inside a furniture store. The owners of the store were justifiably stunned by the verdict since the misbehaving toddler was Mrs. Robertson's *own* son.

- Jerry Williams of Little Rock, Arkansas, received $14,500 and medical expenses when his next door neighbor's beagle bit him on the buttocks. It seems the beagle was on a chain in the owner's fenced yard. The jury gave Mr. Williams less than he sought because they felt the dog might have been provoked by the pellet shots Mr. Williams admitted repeatedly firing at the dog.

- A Philadelphia restaurant was ordered to pay Amber Carson the sum of $113,500 after she slipped on a spilled soft drink and broke her tailbone. It turns out that Ms. Carson herself had thrown the drink at her boyfriend during an argument just 30 seconds before the accident.

- But the prize for winning the best of the outrageous lawsuits of 2002 probably goes to Mr. Merv Grazinski of Oklahoma City. He had just purchased a brand-new, 32-foot Winnebago motor home. On the trip back to his house, he set the cruise control for 70 mph and calmly left the driver's seat to go to the galley to make a cup of coffee. To no one's surprise apparently other than Mr. Grazinski's and the jurors', the vehicle left the freeway, crashed, and overturned. Mr Grazinski sued Winnebago for not advising him in the owner's manual that he couldn't leave the driver's seat while the vehicle was in motion. Mr. Grazinski received $1,750,000 and a new motor home. As a result, Winnebago has actually changed its owner's manual to reflect the findings in the Grazinski case.

If the law is often the best way to solve episodes of uncivil behavior in an urban society, these cases suggest how easily the law can be abused to the detriment of society.

PLAY BALL!

The clash of civility and incivility has become most obvious at professional sporting events. In the United States, a first base coach in a Major League baseball game in Chicago was physically attacked by two men whose motives remain murky. In Oakland, an unruly fan hit a Texas Ranger outfielder in the head with a cell phone. The fan was charged with assault with a deadly weapon!^ But sports anger is a worldwide phenomenon:

- An English soccer fan was sentenced to five years in jail for kung fu kicking the horse of a policeman sent to quell a disturbance between opposing supporters. Worse, the soccer fan was 60 years old and a former usher for the home team!

- In Portsmouth, England, eight fans were arrested for carrying concealed batons and pepper spray to use against fans of the opposing side.

- In Sardinia, a supporter of the home side ran onto the field and punched out the goalkeeper for rival Messina, knocking him unconscious.

- At the Melbourne Cricket Ground in Australia, 300 fans were evicted for disorderly conduct. Eight of the 300 were arrested; "two, unencumbered by clothing, [were taken away for] disporting on the pitch during play."

- The mascot for one Scottish team was threatened with arrest for antagonizing the fans of the opposing side when he simulated the violation of an inflatable sheep in front of them.

CIVILITY

- Supporters for another Scottish team chartered a Boeing 737 for a flight to Spain for their team's match against Celta Vigo. A number of fans were arrested during the match, but the mayhem didn't end there. After takeoff for the return flight to England, a riot started in the back of the plane. The pilot issued a Mayday call, Royal Air Force helicopters were scrambled, and the plane made an emergency landing in Wales. In reporting this incident, Steve Rushin of *Sports Illustrated* could not resist: "The plane from Spain was mainly for the sane." Nevertheless, six people were arrested at the airport in Cardiff.

There is a cure for the danger that unruly sports fans have caused. Stop the contest, divert the television cameras. Rather than leave the decision to referees on the field where the criteria are different, switch the decision to officials in the stands. If fans know that the very event they spent money to see will be canceled for behavior that is dangerous to others, it will cease. Nothing like concentrated peer pressure in a closed environment to cure a problem of incivility.

ABUSES OF OUR CIVILITY

While many of the abuses of civility in America are homegrown, not all the victims, unfortunately, are from this country. Some will remember the crimes committed against foreign tourists to Florida in 2001. The visitors were easily identified in their rental vehicles as they departed Miami International Airport. Soon thereafter, some of them were assaulted, robbed, and shot, prime targets for Miami's criminal element, who knew they likely would be carrying large amounts of cash and would be a lot more civil to people they thought were in some kind of trouble than the racially divided locals.

The problem became so acute that the rental car companies, in cooperation with the Florida tourism authorities and police agencies, issued a list of do's and don'ts to rental customers. Here are some from Hertz's six-language brochure:

- *Always know where you are going and how to get to your destination. If you become lost, do not pull over to the side of the road to read a map or ask for directions. Find a well-lit public area where there are people around.*

- *Avoid traveling in curbside lanes wherever possible. When stopped in traffic, always leave enough room between your car and the one in front so that you can pull around if necessary.*

- *If your car is bumped from behind in a secluded or dark area, do not pull over and stop. Drive to the nearest public area and call for police assistance.*

- *If someone signals you for help, do not stop. Go to a public area and report the incident to the police.*

- *Do not pull over for flashing headlights behind you. Drive to the nearest well-lit public area and check your vehicle.*

We point out this phenomenon to demonstrate that not all of the incivility seen in a modern society is caused by the bad behavior of ordinary people; some of it, clearly, is perpetrated by criminals bent on ignoring the rules of civil behavior.

GOOD MANNERS

While we have said that this book is not about etiquette or manners, we have also pointed out the obvious relationship between common courtesy and civility. Learn courtesy at home, and it is hard to avoid exercising it in public. Take the matter of table manners and their broader meaning. Sue Fox, author of *Etiquette for Dummies,* notes:

> *The premise of table etiquette is courtesy to others. Good manners begin with respect.*^

If someone rests his elbows on a dining table, the body language message is one "of rude indifference. Good posture translates into attentiveness."

In another example of the relationship of the lessons of etiquette to civility, a manners book for kids rightly points out that people are not invited to dinner because the host or hostess thinks the guests might be hungry. Think about that simple truism. You have been invited to dinner for a purpose other than to *eat.* Your job in a private home or at a formal banquet is to first engage your seat neighbors in some kind of conversation. In short, it is bad form in such situations to think only about tucking into the rolls or asking for the butter as your opening attempt at conversation with a seat neighbor.

Etiquette, like civility, is also a lot about common sense. Why is speaking with a mouthful frowned upon? Besides not being very pretty, it avoids the horror of some aspect of what you are eating coming out of your mouth and spraying the person you are speaking to. It could never happen to you? Try saying the word "touching" with a mouthful of chewed nuts or "please" with an almost swallowed lump of raw carrot between your teeth.

SIGNS OF OUR CIVILITY

A survey conducted by Harris Interactive for the makers of Pop-Tarts® looked at the causes of school-day doldrums. The polling firm surveyed a representative geographic sample of kids between the ages of 8 and 18 and asked them to define a bad day at school. Here is how the kids responded.

35%   Not getting along with friends

30%   Not getting good grades

11%   Every day is bad

3%   Not being noticed by someone special

2%   Not wearing the right clothes or accessories

19%   Other problems

While the lead reason—not getting along—may strike some as frivolous, it is probably a good sign for the future of civility in this country. Having friends who care about you and whom you care about is an important attribute of a civil society.

A TWO-WAY STREET

Civility, whenever it occurs, is a two-way street. When someone is acting in an uncivil way in a public setting, turning the other cheek will not make the situation more civil. How one handles a variety of situations hostile to a civil atmosphere is dealt with in the next chapter.

For now, we only make the point that to get civility, you have to give it. In other words, acting in a civil way toward someone else will usually engender a civil response. Just as surely, acting negatively toward the activities of someone else is likely to result in an equally negative response.

THE FINGER

It happened to me the other day. I was on Benedict Canyon Drive, a narrow road through the heart of Beverly Hills that winds its way from the Westside of Los Angeles to the San Fernando Valley. As I came to one of the few traffic lights on this street, I stopped.

I noticed an older car pull up on my right a few moments later. I drive this street nearly every day, and generally anyone creating a second lane at that particular intersection intends to go right. As soon as the light went green, I accelerated forward in what I thought was a normal fashion. The guy on my right didn't. Instead of turning right at the corner, he had obviously pulled alongside to get in *front* of me as soon as the light went green. But he not only was a fraction of a moment late, his car didn't have the power it needed to accomplish his objective.

As I moved forward, I checked my rearview mirror. To my amazement, this guy is on my tail with the middle finger of his right hand in a permanently erect position above his steering wheel. I could only imagine that as soon as he had lost the mini-drag race he had initiated, he raised his salute to my superior driving skill and maintained it until I saw his gesture. When I did, I could only smile. I felt myself totally innocent of any breach of driving etiquette or of any improper behavior. It was to me the perfect symbol of the incivility abroad today.

When has failure to get one's way become a license to insult and berate another person?

PUSHCHAIR AGGRESSION

Here is one more example of how incivility impacts the lives of the civi. Americans call them strollers; the British refer to them as pushchairs. While Americans seem to accept them in shopping malls and amusement parks as well as on long walks from parked cars to ultimate destinations, the British encounter them constantly in the tube, in the streets, in the stores, and on the buses.

To many in England, wielding a stroller can become the equivalent of a terrorist assault. Listen to this description in the London *Telegraph* by Victoria Mather, perhaps not yet a mother herself, of an encounter in a department store.

> *Couples doing their wedding list in china and glass are sundered by the ruthless progress of a [mother and her pushchair]. A Panzer division rarely achieved such an instant return in destruction success. There is also a morbid curiosity, among those not rendered unconscious by having a steel vehicle rammed into their varicose veins, as to why a child capable of walking is being chauffeur-driven.*
>
> *[The driver] is sublimely ungracious. Her smug assertiveness doing wheelies in haberdashery implies her divine right of motherhood. The pushchair, like the cockroach, seemingly has the cunning strength to survive a nuclear holocaust of loathing. Lifts empty at Naomi's approach, only the arthritic remaining pathetically pinned*

against the wall, suppressing apologetic whim-pers as Naomi reverses over their orthopaedic shoes.

Here is the incivility of the mindless. Naomi, the mother, does not even recognize that she is destroying the space and calm of dozens of other people. The telling point is when her little darling in the pushchair calls out, "Mummeee!" in a high-pitched whine. "[Naomi's] parenting classes have taught her that [the child] must be heard, and her verbalisation interpreted in a good way."

So Naomi releases the tormented child from her safety straps.The kid is now free to run about the store and destroy the lives of still others as she careens from rack to gondolier and into changing rooms and behind cash-ier points. The stern calls of her mother are ignored.

Nevertheless, as Mather notes, responding to the kid's demand to leave the pushchair allowed Naomi to con-gratulate "herself on her maternal dedication."

GARBAGE IN, GARBAGE OUT

At a speaking engagement in February 2003, a lady mentioned to me the amount of noise generated and litter left behind by people picking up kids at a school across the street from her house. Her neighbors, she said, were equally outraged at the behavior.

She asked what I would suggest.

As a way to solve the problem, I suggested that she and the neighbors print up a flyer in the form of a questionnaire with a big form at the bottom. The form would ask the individual to provide his or her home address in the space available so that the school's neighbors could bring their garbage for deposit on the visitor's street just as those folks saw fit to leave their garbage behind on the neighbors' streets.

The point is that shaming someone with ridicule is often the best defense against uncivil behavior.

CELL PHONES

On a bus in central London a few months ago, I was stunned to see five people on the lower deck simultaneously engaged in conversations on their "mobiles." I heard one lady discussing where she would be on the weekend, another talking about meeting someone for dinner. I frankly didn't care to share their personal business or the details of their discussions. It sounded to me as if I were in the middle of an old movie showing dozens of switchboard operators sitting on high stools manipulating plugs as they sorted through each incoming and outgoing call to make the appropriate connection.

I later asked a variety of friends about the etiquette of using cell phones in England. There were none, they said. The only time the subject ever comes up apparently is when a phone rings in the cinema or during a West End show. Thoughtless, they all agreed. The attitude seemed to be that the culture expects people to behave in certain settings in specific ways—being quiet in a theater, for example—and that no additional guidance should be necessary.

One Englishman did offer the opinion that he was appalled when a taxi driver took an incoming call and planned a week's holiday in Spain while trying to sort his way through traffic; another said he was behind someone paused in a roadway to turn right, and instead of watching for the instant he could dart through the oncoming traffic, he was bent over his mobile punching in a text message. It seems it's OK to invade the privacy of total strangers on a bus with a cell phone, but not all right to impede another's movement. Very English, it seemed to me.

When I pondered all of this a little further, I realized that since virtually everybody has and uses cell phones in the U.K., no one wants to lose the freedom and convenience that they represent. The English attitude seems to be that it's OK to use a cell phone in public areas if you don't know anyone around you and they don't know you. Where there is a unity of purpose and a clear sharing of values—in a meeting, at a dinner, during a lecture—mobile phone intrusions are condemned.

The fact that the English have not thought it necessary to impose an etiquette on the use of cell phones doesn't mean someone else need shirk the duty. I came to the conclusion that each person should establish his or her own rules for using these instruments until a societal consensus can be achieved to improve civil behavior. (For a discussion of how a societal consensus might be reached, see the discussion of Civility Forums beginning on p. 113.)

For whatever they are worth, here are my cell phone rules:

- When calling to someone's cell phone, always make the first order of business a determination of whether it is a good time to talk. If it is not, identify yourself, and then hang up without fuss or worrying about when he or she might call back.

- When receiving a cell phone call, change the way you respond. Instead of answering "Hello" or with a name, get in the habit of using one of two brief phrases: "Please Go Ahead" to signal that it is an acceptable time to talk or "Please Call Back" if the time or place is not appropriate.

Other thoughts occur on the proper use of cell phones. Just as people ask if it is all right to smoke—an act of courtesy that everyone sensitive to the dangers of second hand smoke appreciates—so those using cell phones in public places—in restaurants, in lines, in stores—should nod or verbalize an apology whenever invading the quiet of someone around them.

If you are bothered by the use of a cell phone and wish privacy, you can always make a hand signal to indicate that the speaker should lower the volume (patting the hand on an imaginery knob in a repeated motion) or that the conversation should end (drawing a forefinger slowly across the throat). Such gestures should be hint enough to return a situation to a level of normalcy.

CIVILITY

DOWN IN FRONT!

I was in England for the London Book Fair. Rather than go directly back to the hotel at the conclusion of the first session on a Sunday, I decided to stop at a pub to watch the last half of a well-anticipated international soccer match on its large screen.

As I settled into a booth with a good, if somewhat distant, view of the action, two men came away from the bar with what was clearly not their first beers of the afternoon. They decided to take up a wide-stance viewing position—to steady themselves against the effects of those previous pints—a few meters in front of my place.

All the coarse American demands I had learned since junior high school came immediately to mind:

- Down in front!
- You make a better door than window!
- Move!
- Do you mind???

Would I dare to use any of these? What is the appropriate etiquette for an English public house? It had been more than 60 years since I was born in England, about 40 years since I had lived there as an adult. Should I merely adjust the demand "Move!" to a more thoroughly British expression they would surely understand: "Clear off!"?

After a while I decided on an approach that I hoped would not cause a scene, offend anyone, and still get my view back. I knew that the first rule of civil behavior in a new situation is to do *nothing* until you have observed everything around you and watched how others act. If that fails to yield any hints of how you should comport yourself, go to Plan B. Plan B is always to ask someone else to help you with your problem.

The second rule of civil behavior is *tone of voice. How* you say something has been demonstrated countless times to be more important than *what* you say. A recent study in England has shown that hand gestures alone make a major difference in what is remembered and what is missed. So think about the word "please." If it comes out as a bitingly sharp **PLEASE!** or a plaintive **PULEEEZE,** it is likely to get someone's back up. If it comes out in a tone that signals a request—**PLEASE?**—it may be just enough to get the desired reaction without stirring any anger or resentment.^

While the situation described above in the English pub was somewhat unusual because it involved finding a civil way to ask for something in a different cultural setting, the problem arises all the time at home as well. Whether it involves a child who cannot see through the individual sitting in front of him or her in a theater or it is an adjustment that needs to be made in a crowd craning to catch a glimpse of a famous person, the request is quite common. Never assume that the other person knows what you may want or hope for. Mind reading was a legendary act in the old days of vaudeville, not a real skill that can produce results in the modern world.

How, then, can you ask someone to move who is blocking your view or the view of someone for whom you are speaking? First remember your objective: It is to get the person in front to move slightly. With that goal in mind, it is not hard to find the right tone in your voice to get the job done. It is when the objective morphs into also showing how powerful you are or how clever you can be that the tone of voice changes into something that can cause the opposite reaction in the listener.

Try some of these concepts in how you might make your request.

CASE STUDIES

Directions	"Perhaps you could shift just a little to the right (or left)."
Question	"Would you mind taking a step to the left (or right)?"
Humor	"If you keep bobbing like that, we're liable to get seasick before the show starts."

Once a person has reacted to your point, be sure to thank him or her for the responsiveness. It will be appreciated, and the dual acts of civility are likely to spread to third parties.

SAY IT AGAIN, SAM

As noted above, one of the keys to civility in our society has nothing to do with the actions taken but the way things are said and the body language that accompanies the words. Verbal and nonverbal signals may do more to set off acts of incivility than all manner of hostile *physical* acts. Because of this, we offer some further thoughts on how things should be presented verbally to minimize the threat that may be implied.

At the outset, consider that no actor thinks about going on stage without rehearsing his part; no athlete competes without first practicing the plays that will be used; no major company offers a new product to the general marketplace without first testing reaction to it. While rehearsal is a common element of so many activities, it never seems to be a major consideration in human interaction. Perhaps people are embarrassed or afraid of sounding less than spontaneous. Whatever the reason, it is nonsense. Rehearsing a conversation before engaging someone in person or on the phone—not only the words but the *tone of voice*—helps insure that the message is conveyed exactly as you desire it and that the listener will not take umbrage at what he or she hears. Secondarily, always listen to your own words during your rehearsals. How would you likely react if someone were saying those same words to you for the first time? If you are honest with yourself, you will be able to make the necessary adjustments.

Sometimes you have no time to rehearse. The situation at hand calls for an immediate reaction. So use this time now to test how you might handle the following sudden situations:

- Pretend you come across someone who has been hurt in a car accident. The person is trapped inside the car. After ascertaining what professional help might be needed and what you might be able to do until the help arrives, what do you say to the person? What would you find comforting in these circumstances? What do you think *your* minister would say to you?

- Someone is about to pour the remnants of a can of motor oil into a street gutter. You know that the oil will eventually migrate to the sewer system and onward to the ocean where it can do damage to the environment. What do you say to the individual to stop him without getting into a war with the individual?

- You notice a little kid carrying packages for a lady struggling to get herself and her walker across a broad boulevard before a light that never seems long enough changes. You are pleased to see that everyone arrives on the other sidewalk in one piece despite the visible impatience of the drivers waiting to proceed. The kid deserves praise for his act of kindness. How do you convey it?

WHAT'S GOOD FOR THE GOOSE ...

What's good for the goose may not always be right for the gander. Take how trust is exhibited in society in the case of payments for a product or service.

- In a fast-food restaurant such as McDonald's, payment for the food is expected before the requested items are gathered from the holding trays; in others, such as Subway, a sandwich is made or food is prepared before payment is sought. But in any sit-down restaurant—from a coffee shop to a white linen establishment—food is ordered, prepared, and consumed long before a request for payment is made.

- In the case of the publishing industry, payment for a sale of books to a brick-and-mortar bookseller will likely occur 90 days *after* the books are received; but payment for a sale over the Internet usually must clear the processing bank *before* a book is shipped.

- In England, passengers board a bus and take their seats long before the conductor arrives to ask them for the money. The fare to be paid, moreover, is determined by the individuals' honesty in correctly identifying their starting points and ending stops. In the United States, passengers are required to pay for their passage before taking a seat, and it is usually a fixed fare.

- Doctors used to bill patients at the end of the month in which the treatment was rendered; now

CIVILITY

71

patients are requested to pay for their care at the end of their visit to the office.

- Of course some payments are made before and after goods are purchased or a service is rendered. In the case of a product specially ordered, a deposit is usually required to show the intent to complete a transaction. In the case of tipping, while usually done *after* service is rendered, the smart money knows that when tips are given at the outset of a cruise or when something is requested of a maid in a hotel room, it is a signal that more might be coming and usually insures even greater attention.

- When all gasoline was pumped by an attendant, the gas and other services were done before costs were assessed and payment requested; in a world of self-service functions, payment is now demanded before the gasoline can be dispensed from the pump.

What has happened here? Has the world become more distrustful or have we become more efficient? It is probably a little of both. But it is also a function of the growth and impersonalization of society today. When suppliers and providers knew all of their customers, most had a pretty sound idea of the credit worthiness of their patrons and could provide goods and services accordingly. Today, as society has become larger, more mobile, and more insular, trust evaporates in a fog of the unknown.

"DO IT TRUE"

The director of a Susan Sarandon/Goldie Hawn 2002 film, *The Banger Sisters*, portrays a high school graduation audience. Parents, teachers, counselors, and friends are enraptured when the class valedictorian proclaims that others have always set goals for her life: "Go to college, make money, have a family." The valedictorian notes that in following this advice, she has lost track of herself. She then tells her classmates:

Whatever you do, do it true, do it true.

The scene then switches back to the audience, and they are shown on their feet, smiling, clapping, cheering. Amazing. They are not only denigrating their own teachings, but they are applauding American high school education for helping kids discover an amazing intellectual fact: *Truth* is important. While some would read her command to "Do it true" to be a restatement of the Shakespearean injunction "To thine own self be true," others see it as a justification for selfishness: "Do it your way and to hell with the impact it has on others."

A more intriguing issue with the command "Do it true" is to what extent *truth* can actually be ascertained. Philosophers have been wrestling with that concept for millenniums. A case in point is the lead paragraph in a story in *The Wall Street Journal* on how differently the same day of the war in Iraq was seen by America's Cable News Network (CNN) and Qatar's al-Jazeera television network:

On Thursday, March 27 [2003] at six in the morning in the U.S., two in the afternoon in Baghdad, CNN showed paratroopers jump from a plane to open the northern front in Iraq. On al-Jazeera, a little Iraqi girl in a pink sweater stares out from her Baghdad hospital bed.

Because truth can be seen so differently by so many people, civility demands humility, patience, and a willingness to see the other person's point of view. Absolutes, of course, cannot be excluded, but they should not be assumed based on cultural, geographic, or demographic generalizations or perspectives.

CASE STUDIES

ON DEATH

How people die and how their remains are treated thereafter is one of the key measures used to determine if a particular society meets Western standards of civility. And, of course, not all Western societies agree among themselves on these topics. Even more, there is considerable dispute *within* many societies on such matters as assisted suicide and euthanasia.

But perhaps the most bizarre example of an issue involving death occurred recently in the U.S. federal appeals court in St. Louis. There, officials of the Arkansas prison system were finally given permission to force a prisoner to take antipsychotic medication to make him eligible to be executed! Judge Roger L. Wollman noted that the court had to choose between medication and execution and no medication and psychosis. The majority of judges felt the drugs were generally beneficial to the prisoner and ought to be administered. Wollman then added dryly and apparently with no sense of irony: "Eligibility for execution is the only unwanted consequence of the medicine."

Judge Gerald W. Heany dissented. He said: "To execute a man who is severely deranged without treatment, and arguably incompetent when treated is what [former Supreme Court] Justice [Thurgood] Marshall called 'the barbarity of exacting mindless vengeance.'" While the 6-5 decision stands, the issue of whether this treatment is a civilized extension of the death penalty is sure to be revisited.

NO THANKS NEEDED

Jewish burial societies perform a necessary service to their communities. The societies are formed to do whatever is necessary to care for a person's body within the prescribed time between death and interment. Members of burial societies are particularly honored by the community because they give of themselves without the possibility of any reward of any kind from the deceased.

Think about the power of *that* historic concept in terms of building a higher level of civility within our society. What if everyone you knew…

**Did things because they are right to do,
not in anticipation of any praise or appreciation.**

Here is just a partial list of what that might involve.

- Pick up paper on sidewalks or lawns whenever found in a residential neighborhood.

- Remove a branch or other debris from a secondary road instead of driving around it.

- Ask a parent to keep his or her kids out of the flower beds in a public park.

- Close a door in a conference or meeting to prevent outside distractions and preserve privacy.

No request, no reward. Simple. Clean. Yet intensely satifying, civil, and ultimately beneficial to all.

CIVILITY:
SITUATIONS AND SOLUTIONS

INTRODUCTION

Here we hope to challenge your appreciation of civility by providing a variety of situations and asking you how you might react to them. Our hope is that by putting your newly gained understanding of civility to the test, you will be more comfortable and more spontaneous when next faced with a similar situation requiring a reaction. Practicing in the safe environment of your own space and according to your own timetable cannot help but make you feel more comfortable. When confronted, you can have that "been there, done that" feeling.

Please note that our suggested responses are just that—*suggestions*. They are by no means either the *only* answer or the *correct* one. They are simply what the military terms the "school" answer—a response that has the luxury of long consideration and multiple vettings to arrive at something suitable to the circumstances. Take the responses, then, as *starting* points for adjusting them to fit your own personality and the actual conditions you encounter.

To help you in formulating your responses, here is a list of principles of civil behavior that may guide your reaction to any of the situations we describe.

Shame   Shame usually works in improving civility when there is a major age disparity between the person causing the incivility and the individual suffering its results.

Humor   One of my father's favorite ways of complaining about being knocked about in a queue, on a dance floor, or by a crowd was to turn to the person who had bumped into him with a question: "Isn't the state of California big enough so that you and I don't have to be in the same place at the same time?" It usually evoked a smile, a hurried "Sorry!" and a little more care in moving about.

Golden Rule   Use a variant of the famous moral lesson: *Do* **for** *me what you would expect* **from** *me.*

Health   Most people are solicitous of health problems. So in registering a complaint (about an odor, say) or making a request (about smoking in a restricted area), ask the person to refrain from doing whatever is being done because: "My doctor says it is harmful to (my, your, or someone else's) health."

Comparison Ask the offending individual if he would want some statement said in front of *his* mother, or would he want *his* son to see that kind of behavior?

Forgiveness Introduce any intervention with a disarming request signaling obeisance: "Forgive me for interrupting, but ..."

Kindness Another variation of the forgiveness technique involves expressing a request to stop some bothersome behavior with a statement like: "I know you are just having fun or are discussing something important, but would you mind terribly (if you carried on outside, in the hall, or put a comma there until we leave).

Ask for What You Want Don't expect other people to read your mind. They probably don't know they're bothering you with their behavior. Verbalize your request to them in a polite and respectful manner.

News at 11 When a group of people is behaving poorly in public with loud or raucous behavior, try asking them to visualize their reaction if they saw themselves on television. While this can cause a moment of additional antics, it can also be sufficient to get them to eventually halt the offending behavior.

Be Selective   There are more problems in the world than any one person can solve. Don't try. Save your energy for those that are most important to you. You will be more effective on *your* issues, and others will be more dedicated when dealing with theirs.

Wait   Before plunging into any situation that is bothering you, pause long enough to be sure you understand all of its dimensions. It saves embarrassment, and another moment to appreciate all the ramifications of your action won't matter that much.^

As a general rule you will be much more effective whenever seeking to correct some bothersome public behavior if you always try to practice what you preach. For example, if you react viscerally when someone tosses a half-filled cup of latte out of a moving car, then the next time you have a cellophane candy wrapper needing disposal, do it in the proper receptacle rather than "accidently" dropping it as the door of the car opens.

Finally, remember that standards change just as fashions and language do. What you remember from 50 years ago is probably not appropriate in today's world. For example, men used to wear hats, not caps, to baseball games, and women wore gloves when going out, not jeans and a T-shirt. Expressions involving the word screw ("screw you, screwed up") were forbidden in days gone by because everyone knew it was a way of disguising the use of the "F-word." Now, of course, the "F-word" is heard more frequently in everyday speech, on cable television, and emblazoned on shirts.

As a result, whenever making a suggestion to someone else about his or her behavior in an effort to increase the level of civility in a community, be sure it is appropriate to the situation and conditions in today's world. If you are not sure, always phrase your request as a question ("Wouldn't it be better for both of us if …?"), and see what kind of response you get.

THE ROLE OF RESPECT
The Situation

Civility is strongly rooted in respect for the views, needs, and interests of others with whom we share public space. If each person thinks to give respect to others, it is likely that he or she will get respect in return.

Simple premise, but sometimes difficult to achieve. It is reminiscent of something we wrote about in a book called *Concentration.* As we noted in the Introduction, a lot of people talk about the need for concentration in various situations, but very few have ever tried to analyze *how* the skill can be developed in kids or adults. Kennith Harris and I used a mock newspaper article about an imaginary car accident to point out.

> *[T]he importance of focusing the mind when involved in a difficult, repetitious, or boring activity. While a lot has been done to improve memory, particularly for the elderly, concentration is a different skill that, in fact, underlies the ability to remember. Lack of concentration is a problem, not only when driving a car, but while sitting in a class, talking with a group, watching a show, playing a game, or doing anything else.*

By the same token, giving and receiving *respect* are easy to talk about but difficult to achieve. Essentially it is the effort to avoid behavior that will knowingly shock, offend, or embarrass someone else. Now put it positively: How do you show respect for a stranger whether encountered in a line, on a sidewalk, or in a hall?

CIVILITY

83

THE ROLE OF RESPECT
The Solution

Here are some positive ways we think people can show respect for others … and thus receive respect in return.

Listen Give the other person's words importance by paying careful attention to them.

Value Give the other person's position worth by coming to terms with the basis on which it rests.

Status Recognize the size and condition of the larger group that holds different views from yours.

Sometimes, putting the rules in a negative framework makes them easier to adopt. In other words, don't ridicule, mock, or dismiss the views of others. Don't disagree blatantly: "That's wrong!" Instead, try asking a question: "Could you have missed something?" Rather than the command "Don't touch," try "What happens if it breaks?"

Someone once summed up showing respect as not taking what is not yours, giving credit to others, and getting attention from good deeds rather than negative ones.

SITUATIONS/SOLUTIONS

MAKING CONVERSATION
The Situation

It seems that incivility occurs more often when the people involved are at arm's length from each other— unseen and unheard directly. By the same token, civility may be said to *begin* when people communicate with each other. Communication starts with conversation. If we want to build a stronger civilization, then we need to do a better job of teaching young people the art of making conversation. Most people never learn it; no one seems to teach it.^

We want to rectify the matter now. Pretend a colleague of yours finds himself among total strangers in one of the following situations:

- A reception for the secretary of State

- A banquet to aid the Stroke Association

- Floor seats at Staples Center next to Jack Nicholson

- Leaving your car to see what is happening in a massive traffic jam where nothing has moved in 20 minutes

How do you tell your colleague to initiate a conversation with the first person encountered in any of these particular situations?

MAKING CONVERSATION
The Solution

The technique for initiating a conversation in any of the situations described above is remarkably the same.

The first rule of good conversation is deciding what information you want to get or impart. As a result, you are really not interested in hearing about the other person's views on the weather, a political position, or where the individual lives within the community.

Good conversation starts with getting the other person to open up. Ask the other individual how he or she comes to be at this place at this time or how a particular event will affect their immediate lives. If the other person is equally adept at conversation, know to make your answers brief and turn the questions back to the other person as quickly as possible. If names have not come up in the first few minutes, be sure to introduce yourself and ask for the same information from the other person. Always have a few questions in the back of your mind that elicit *feelings*. They tend to keep a conversation going, reveal a lot about the other person, do not need facts to sustain or challenge a conclusion, and can spark a response no matter what is said: "The last time I felt that way ..." and you are off.

HANDLING A CONVERSATION
The Situation

If civility starts with conversation—as we assert—so maintaining a civil attitude must be dependent on handling a difficult conversation. Take the following situation:

> You are at a one-day conference for gold investors. While sipping coffee and waiting for the doors to a meeting room to open, you fall into conversation with another individual standing close by. After a few moments, you determine that he has been in and out of the gold market for a long time. Perfect. You decide to ask him whether he has any explanation for the fact that the price of gold barely moved during the Persian Gulf War in 1991 but proved to be highly volatile during the Iraq War in 2003.

You see from his identification badge that his name is David Colton; you know your last name—Eliaspour—is difficult for some, so you ask him to call you Steve. As David warms to the theme you have offered, he somehow digresses into a story about an Iranian businessman who cheated him years ago and then launches into a description of his other experiences with "Farsi-speaking Persian punks" who would cheat their own mothers if they could tell which one was theirs under all the jewelry "those people" wear.

You are taken aback. He has either not paid any attention to your surname or assumed it to be French, not someone whose parents come from Teheran.

87

HANDLING A CONVERSATION
The Solution

Some people will tell you that the easiest way to avoid uncomfortable conversations with strangers who may reveal hidden prejudices or deep hatreds is not to start them in the first place. A second line of defense involves signaling the kind of topics or themes that you will not be comfortable exploring with strangers: "I sure hope we don't have to talk about the Dodgers"—or the "Bush administration," or whatever.

My own approach is to let a conversation unfold and then try to control it if it becomes uncomfortable. For example, when another person is using a lot of bad language, I will try a comment such as: "I don't mind, but your words may bother others. I bet your vocabulary is big enough to find less abrasive ways to say things." Flattery with or without a soft rebuke is usually good enough to maintain civility. If the other person starts to veer toward criticizing another ethnic or religious group—"I have a real aversion to pushy Jehovah Witnesses when they pester you"—I usually respond with: "Oh, we have some Witnesses in our office, and not all of them are that aggressive in their missionary work." Often a fact or personal experience will triumph over an ill-defined feeling or unsubstantiated bias. Finally, civility can be maintained by using someone else's diatribe as a learning experience. Rather than take umbrage at every slur, listen, tell the other person ambiguously that his point is "interesting," and excuse yourself to go to the restroom.

AT A PUBLIC MEETING
The Situation

At the public meeting in the hall of the local recreation center, the crowd was restless as the Coastal Commission chairman carefully worked his way through a long agenda filled with announcements of commemorative events in the ensuing month, appreciations for other political leaders about to retire, a bevy of personnel decisions pending, and such administrative issues as the timing of the next budget. Boring. Tedious.

The hot-button issue that the crowd was there to protest seemed to be more than an hour away. The chairman clearly was in no rush to get there. The lawyers and political consultants for the developers, all staunch supporters of the chairman, were seeking approval to build a hotel on a gently sloping bluff overlooking the ocean in an area that had no such facility. Everyone but the first-timers in the audience knew that the later the meeting lasted, the more people would drift away and fewer statements, other than those of commissioners, could be made, edited, and reported on the 10:00 and 11:00 news programs.

You are there representing a group anxious to insure that any approval involves assurances from the hotel management that public access to the beach will be both convenient and unrestricted. The later it gets, the more restless the crowd becomes. Everyone is now heckling. How do you proceed?

AT A PUBLIC MEETING
The Solution

There are several standard ways to promote civility in public meetings, whether part of the authority convening the meeting or as a member of the audience.

- Adhering to well-known or well-accepted rules of procedure is usually the best way to control audiences and/or insure that a discussion proceeds in an orderly manner.

- Taking lots of time to discuss the noncontroversial elements of an agenda before a hot-button issue arises usually takes some of the fight out of an audience and the anger out of the ensuing discussion.

- If the laws of physics hold that any action generates an equal and opposite reaction, so the laws of politics suggest that any hostility evidenced by a political body will be met by at least an equal amount of bad blood from another group. As a result, unfailing politeness, patience, and respect for the audience—as part of it or as an official—usually promote calm, reasonable, and respectful responses from them.

AT THE THEATER
The Situation

You have settled into your seat, and the usual tingle of anticipation grips you as it does every time you are about to experience a play or a film that you have looked forward to seeing. It is the expectation of being dazzled, surprised, shocked, and/or excited. It is an expectation that comes from your childhood when your parents used to take you to the theater but never told you what you were going to see or what to expect.

In the row directly behind you are two teenage girls. They are chatting away to each other when you hear one of their cell phones ring: "Hello" one says. "Who is it?" the other one insists. "Bill!" the first girl announces with some excitement. "Oh, well, aren't we the privileged one" the other one says in a very stagey voice. "Shuuush," the one on the phone commands, "I can't hear what he is saying." "Major shame," the other shoots back, sitting forward in her seat, half in jealousy, half in anticipation of analyzing what Bill really wants.

At that instant, the lights go down, the curtain starts to rise, and the screen lights up. But absolutely nothing changes from the row behind. The one on the telephone is totally oblivious to the screen, to the audience around her, and the conversation plays on.

What do you do to correct this situation?

AT THE THEATER
The Solution

The talker-in-the-theater problem is widespread. Some people simply can't stop a conversation in midsentence; others feel compelled to show their triumphant superiority to neighbors and the whole world around them by talking through the credits, announcements, trailers, and advertisements. Because you are concerned for your own comfort and enjoyment in these situations, you want the disturbance to end with the least amount of tension. As a result, we advocate a form of escalated diplomacy, a series of steps that control the level of your involvement with each succeeding gesture.

Step 1   Raise the back of your hand above the height of the seat to signal a stop. If they continue talking …

Step 2   Raise the back of your hand above the back of the seat and waggle it gently from side to side. If they continue talking …

Step 3   Turn in your seat and provide them with the traditional vertical forefinger in front of the lips. If they continue talking …

Step 4   Ask them to be quiet with a single word: **PLEASE.** If this request does not help, or they say something rude back …

Step 5   Summon the manager and demand that they be removed from their seats.

WAITING IN LINE
The Situation

It's 2:00 in the afternoon and your post office has a long line. Only one clerk is on duty. You have a number of transactions to complete, you have other errands to do, and you have promised to be home at 4:30. As you take your place in line, you can feel the stress surging through your body.

It builds as the line moves glacially forward. The clerk keeps asking questions of additional services she might provide instead of finishing with customers as quickly as possible. Can it be that you have been inching forward for 40 minutes and yet are still two people away from being attended to? Finally, the individual in front of you moves to the counter. You are next.

At that moment a lady comes into the Post Office clutching a telltale blue-and-white Priority mailer. She ignores the line and marches straight to the counter. You can't hear the conversation with the clerk, but you see she is distraught as she turns away. To ease the tension, you say to no one in particular: "Well the line is a lot shorter than when I came in." She stops, then blurts out: "Excuse me. I hate to ask this, but I really need to get this to Miami. It's a proposal that means a great deal and it has to be there by Monday. The last pickup for Priority Mail is 3:00. He told me to wait my turn. Do you think you might let me go in front of you?"

How do you respond?

WAITING IN LINE
The Solution

If civility is to rule in our communities, you have to recognize when you really have no choice. This is one of those occasions. You accept the little added delay in your own schedule in order to feel good about yourself and about doing a favor for someone who needs a favor. It is one of those acts of kindness that has no greater reward than a thank you and a smile.

The next time you have the chance to do such a favor for a complete stranger, do it. See how you feel. Even though doing the favor might put you at a momentary disadvantage, note that doing something for someone else reduces your stress level, increases your feeling of well-being, and improves your disposition.

It works. We urge you to try.

BEFORE OPENING HOURS
The Situation

It's Sunday morning and you have been given a dozen tasks by your wife for your "melon list"—"honey do this, honey do that." But you need to pick up some supplies at the hardware store before getting to the market. So you bribe the first sleepy kid you see with the promise of a donut stop and drive off to the Do It Yourself corner of the shopping mall, planning your arrival there for a few seconds before the 9:00 opening.

But as you pull into the parking lot, you see a knot of people milling around the front entrance. Oops! Opening time has been changed to 9:30. Happens. But what to do? Return home and come back? Sit in the car and mope? Get out and join the waiting throng? You choose the latter. It is a chance to stretch your legs and perhaps show one of your children what it takes to make a civil society thrive.

That's the question. What can you do with this random opportunity to help build a more civil society?

BEFORE OPENING HOURS
The Solution

Civil societies are not created in a vacuum. It takes interaction among the individuals of a community to find the common ground of behavior and attitudes in public that they find acceptable and comfortable. So one of the most significant lessons any parent or grandparent can teach a youngster is the importance of finding opportunities to discuss societal topics of potential mutual interest with neighbors. Waiting around for a local store to open is a perfect such occasion. People are all there for a similar purpose, are generally not distracted by other concerns at that moment, no doubt live in the vicinity, and have as much interest in the well-being of the community as you do.

So use the opportunity to let your opinions and attitudes start filtering through the community. Make it a point to start a conversation. Engage your child in the process. Pick out something unusual or noteworthy about another person's attire, accessories, or attitude and remark to them about it: "Does your shirt tell me you are in the Army or you have a kid serving?" "Billy, I have to ask what that tool is used for?" "Do you think it's right that people aren't allowed to take their dogs into stores?"

Once the conversation is under way, you can guide it to what's in the news or any other topic that energizes you or elicits some opinion or a feeling from the other person.

IN A PUBLIC FACILITY
The Situation

A grandfather was in the Men's room at a basketball arena when he saw a little boy, perhaps four years old, emerge from a toilet stall. When the boy's father, waiting impatiently near the entrance, spotted him, he yelled: "Come on, Jimmy, we gotta go. The game's going to start and I wanna get a beer before we go up to the seats." The little boy responded plaintively, "But I haven't washed my hands yet."

"Give me a break," the father barked in an exasperated voice that suggested that following Mom's rules in a man's world was wimpy. "We're going now!"

The grandfather, fearing this walking biohazard might leave infectious agents behind on everything the boy would touch, had only a moment to decide what to do.

Interfering with a father's authority is never welcomed— especially given this one's build, mood, and demeanor— but particularly abhorred by a stressed-out person who might react irrationally. By the same token, the grandfather felt his civic responsibilities demanded that he protect others from unseen but potential danger.

In an instant, he decided what he would do. Turn the page to learn the action this grandfather took.

IN A PUBLIC FACILITY
The Solution

The grandfather decided to wet a paper towel and hand it to the boy's father. He merely said: "Maybe this will solve the problem and save all of us from catching something we don't need."

The father took the towel, mumbled a begrudging "thank you," and could be seen swiping at the kid's hands as they rushed away toward the closest food stand.

GENDER CONFUSION
The Situation

You are in an airport, waiting for a friend to emerge from a flight from Washington, D.C. Your friend's plane has landed but has not yet taxied to the gate. As you hang back, just watching the flow of human traffic to and around the gate, you notice an old man approach the restrooms to your left. You also note that the maintenance crew has posted an orange cone and a sign announcing that the Men's room is closed for cleaning. The old man seems utterly confused by the situation. He is also in some obvious discomfort. Can you help?

CIVILITY

GENDER CONFUSION
The Solution

Clearly, you can help in a number of ways. You could find out how long the cleanup crew will be in the bathroom. You could find out where the next nearest Men's room is located. You could ask the cleanup crew to see if the Ladies' room might be used in an emergency. All take energy, and you don't know, at that stage, how much time you might have before your friend arrives; you don't even know if you can communicate with the old man, particularly if he speaks a foreign language. As a result, most of us would rather just watch and turn away, leaving the solution to someone else or letting some small disaster unfold.

We hold that when this occurs, civilization is worse off. If each of us acted on our impulses and did what is right and what is needed at that moment, we would live in a much more civil society.

WHAT IS IT ABOUT GOLF?
The Situation

Golf may well be the most difficult of all individual sports. Every time players go to the first tee on a golf course, they face a host of conditions likely not to have been faced before. Forget the fact that they may be playing on a course new to them or on a familiar course that has been altered. Even if they think they are as familiar with a course as they are with their own gardens, they know that the natural conditions they will face change each time they play—the sun is making different shadows, the wind is coming at a different speed from a different angle, a maturing leaf interferes with a ball's projected flight, even the grass itself is at a different height or been damaged by a divot. In short, the nature of golf is that it challenges players with a new set of circumstances each time they set out to hit a ball during each round of golf they play.

The difficulty of golf is also matched by the rigors of its rules. They are exacting, severe, and self-enforcing. If you play golf, you are expected by everyone—and most especially yourself—to obey the rules. Every other sport features uniformed referees. They determine whether a rule has been transgressed, whether the players are competing fairly. As a result, how many times have you seen players trying to get away with a little cheat—pulling a shirt, holding an opponent, blocking a view? How many times do you see a player admit to a foul or seek to override a referee's call? It is somewhere between seldom (tennis) and never (soccer).

WHAT IS IT ABOUT GOLF?
The Solution

Golf is as exacting as it is a learning experience for life. Deepak Chopra, one of the principal philosophers of New Age thinking, has a new book called *Golf for Enlightenment* in which he declares that golf "has the ability to bring out the truth about a person almost immediately."

An organization called First Tee helps kids learn to play golf. But as First Tee notes in its television advertising, golf is not just about the proper grip, the correct swing, the right clothing, the appropriate equipment, and the intelligent management of a course.

Golf, First Tee suggests, is about the lessons of life that will stand any player long into the future: It is about obeying the rules, being honest, keeping your own score, repairing a ball mark for the benefit of other players, waiting your turn, being quiet, standing still, not walking in someone else's putting line, and more.

Think about teaching the values of golf to kids, and you are talking about a better society in the future. As the ad's tag line suggests: "Put golf in people's lives and watch them grow." We would add, "And watch society improve."

AT THE HOTEL
The Situation

Out of nowhere a door bangs, two people are shouting at each other, and still more people seem to be laughing. I am in a hotel room in London. The noise wakes me. I flip on the light to see my watch: 3:30AM. Clearly the party was still going on for these people, but where exactly are they—next door, in the hall, on the street below? More questions flit through my mind: Do I really have the energy to find out? Are they speaking English or is that muffled sound some foreign language? Are they really talking about running out of drink before they run out of energy? Mercifully, I fall back to sleep while contemplating all of these mind-sapping options only to wake two hours later because of the same source. I decide to get up, take a shower, and decide what to do.

Nothing perhaps is more uncivil than when public space is invaded by inconsiderate people involved only in their own activities. What might you have done in the circumstances?

AT THE HOTEL
The Solution

Excessive noise in a hotel room is clearly an example of civil behavior being forgotten in a place and at a time that clearly demands something different. Any facility shared temporarily with strangers requires sensitivity to the situation. In our culture, most guests in an urban hotel are expected to be asleep a few hours before dawn. These louts had no worry how their noise was affecting those around them; they carried on as if they were in the middle of Hyde Park at high noon with only a few odd squirrels to be concerned about.

The most immediate solution in such a situation is to engage the hotel's security staff. But without knowing the source of a disturbance, it would do no good. So I decided I could do nothing. Then as luck would have it, one of the party people emerged into the hall in search of the ice machine as I was leaving my room for breakfast. Instantly I opened up: "You really have to do a better job at making noise; I managed a whole hour of sleep last night." At first she looked like a deer caught in the headlights, then her face relaxed as she turned to dart back into the safety of her room and the arms of her friends. The smile was my reward. The point was made but with enough gentle humor to insure that she would discuss it without all of them deciding to adopt a belligerent attitude that might make the next night even worse. To reinforce the point that it is not *what* you say but *how* you say it that counts, I did not hear a further peep from that neighboring room for the rest of my stay.

CIGARETTE CINDY
The Situation

You are sitting in one of the airport lounges in Miami International Airport, relaxing in a nonsmoking area while you wait for your flight to be called.

Just as you are about to open your book to read, you notice a woman hurriedly enter the lounge, looking clearly agitated. She heads straight in your direction. As she nervously looks around—is this some kind of terrorist action?—she plops herself down near a table outfitted with a phone. But instead of finding out how to use *that* instrument, she whips out a cell phone and begins the laborious process of thumbing her way through the recorded address book looking for a number. With her other hand, she begins to frantically rummage around in her handbag for a cigarette. She is sitting underneath the NO SMOKING sign but is clearly oblivious to the prohibition and may not take kindly to any instructions from you. Does she speak English? Do you want a scene? Is it worth the effort to go into action? What harm will one cigarette do?

After deciding your own response to the situation, turn the page to see what we did in this situation.

CIVILITY

CIGARETTE CINDY
The Solution

Not knowing her mental state or her language capability, we decided on pantomime. As the cigarette emerged from the handbag, she set it down on the table next to the phone. Then we saw her left hand dive back into the depths of the handbag, this time clearly in search of a lighter or matches.

First we waggled our finger at her in a horizontal wave to get her attention and to suggest that what she was about to do was not permitted. She caught the waggle out of the corner of her eye and looked up perplexed. Ah, we thought, she knew exactly where she had chosen to sit and she had seen the NO SMOKING sign. She smiled softly as she relaxed her shoulders—body language that indicated submission—then held up her finger in a return pantomime as if to signal "for a brief moment." We interpreted the request as having to do with finding her lighter. We were then surprised to see that it really meant she wanted a moment to smoke her cigarette and that she was asking for our permission to break the rules of the room.

This was a woman who appeared to be used to getting her own way. Fine. But a public place, where the rules of civility require her to be as conscious of our needs as she was of her own, demanded different behavior. So we waggled our finger more forcefully and pointed to the sign. At that, she merely shrugged, gathered up her belongings, and went in search of a place in the confined and crowded smoking area.

GAS-POWERED BLOWERS
The Situation

You have decided that this will be the day to stay home from the office to get some serious work done. You look forward to these times when there are no appointments, no hurried meetings, no telephone calls, no interruptions of staff, no time wasted in inane chat in the coffee room.

Just as you sit down at your laptop, you hear the *froooom, froooom* of a gas-powered leaf blower fire up. You decide to ignore it. *Froooom, Froooom, Froooom.* The operator is clearly a frustrated Formula One driver, and while checking on the firing sequence of a race-car engine makes some sense, a sudden increase in the engine revolutions of a leaf blower has no purpose. What if it misfires? If one leaf remains behind while the others are pushed on their way to a gathering point, will something actually be lost, will someone suffer? Clearly not. It is merely a "driver" entertaining himself with the sounds and rhythms he is generating.

But if you are to have peace and quiet so that you can achieve your goals for the day, you have to do something. What do you do?

CIVILITY

GAS-POWERED BLOWERS
The Solution

In this case, you have two objectives. One is to get the gardener to stop revving the engine, and the other is to get the leaf blowing confined to a known schedule.

With the lady of the house—your neighbor—you do not want confrontation. In this case, it is always better to ask questions such as

- Could you ask the gardeners to limit the leaf blowing to no more than five minutes?

- Might we make an agreement on exactly when they will operate their leaf blowers? Then I know to do other things so that the noise is not so disturbing.

As a final act of courtesy, you might always consider ending these kinds of discussions—those that put the other person at any kind of inconvenience—with a question of whether there is anything happening at your house that might be bothersome. For example, you could offer to correct the odors emanating from the barbeque, turn down a loud television, or switch off a light that shines too brightly.

AT THE WAREHOUSE STORE
The Situation

We went shopping at one of the big warehouse stores the other day, filled up a basket with large quantities of products and groceries at what we thought were good prices, and then went in search of the fastest-moving checkout line. We were late for our baby-sitting chores.

Finding a fast-moving line in some of these stores is not always an easy task. But we knew that sometimes lines longer in length dissipate more rapidly if the amount to be purchased per person is small. When we saw one person using a credit card to buy a case of wine and another clutching a shirt behind someone maneuvering a large flatbed cart, we knew where we should queue. To make conversation while waiting, I said to the older man holding the shirt that he should ask the lady with the flatbed cart if he could go in front of her. He said he was hoping she would recognize that he had a quick transaction and *invite* him to go before her. He added that it was his way of testing people's attitudes.

Given the fact that she was trying to maneuver the cart and deal with a one-year-old baby's needs, it was clear the man did not know how to ask for what he wanted. So I whispered to him the magic words to use. What do you think they were?

AT THE WAREHOUSE STORE
The Solution

I told the guy that if he states his case clearly and simply: "Would you mind if I go in front of you? I have just this one item and I will be paying cash," the other person will find it impossible to refuse his request. She didn't. In fact, she was very sweet about it. She said that she often asks the same favor of strangers and always appreciates it when they accede.

The man was very pleased and thanked me for giving him the courage to ask. I told him that in the future he should remember that the worst that could happen is someone's not understanding the request because of language problems or telling him that they themselves were in a rush and really couldn't spare the time. I said that in that case you will be no worse off than you are now if you hadn't asked—waiting.

The lesson is simple. People are generally civil and friendly, and when asked in the right way, they will be as accommodating as possible in the circumstances. Remember the rule: Always ask for what you want.

ACTS OF CIVILITY
The Situation

American culture, particularly, has a somewhat ambivalent attitude toward certain activities of its citizens. The question is whether any of the following situations promote or hinder the improvement of civil behavior in the society:

- You enter a convenience store intent on buying a lottery ticket for the next regular drawing. While you are selecting your numbers, you notice another patron stuffing two candy bars into her backpack. Do you say anything, and if you decide to say something, to whom do you say it?

- A severe windstorm strikes your neighborhood. It knocks over a neighbor's tree, which dents the roof and hood of his car. Your neighbor later tells you that the insurance company is going to cover the damage, even to the dent in the fender that you know was there long before the windstorm. Do you say anything, and if you decide to say something, to whom do you say it?

- You go with a cousin to take the written portion for a driver's license. In the middle of the test you notice he is looking at notes he made to help him remember the difference between certain painted lines on the street. Do you say anything, and if you decide to say something, to whom do you say it?

ACTS OF CIVILITY
The Solution

Despite the fact that all the cases described are different, the observer is put in exactly the same position. He is faced with the American dilemma: Does he tell someone in authority that cheating is occurring, or does he ignore what he knows in order to avoid involvement and getting someone else into trouble.

If he identifies the cheating to authorities, the hope arises that such behavior will discourage others and that the cost of goods and services will be reduced. But American culture abhors getting friends and relatives in trouble; people who snitch, tattle, rat-on, or otherwise make life difficult for someone close to them are considered the scum of the earth, low-life snakes who use such underhanded means to gain personal advantage. By the same token, identifying a complete stranger who is engaged in some act of cheating is considered heroic. After all, the observer has put himself in potential jeopardy by getting someone else in trouble.

In the interest of creating a more civil society, how are the two attitudes reconciled? We suggest that observers do *not* differentiate between those they know and those they don't. In both cases, we recommend that the observer pose a question to the cheat. Did you forget you put the candy away? Do you really believe the tree could have dented the fender as well? If you can't remember for a test, how will you be able to remember while you are driving? Questions save face and leave the ultimate guilt with the perpetrator, not you.

SITUATIONS/SOLUTIONS

112

CIVILITY
FORUMS

CIVILITY FORUMS

We would argue that given the deteriorating state of civility in many communities and given the common belief that cheats often do in fact prosper, our society needs to establish a new way to determine what is acceptable civil behavior for the majority of people in the same community. Too often, the reaction of some to polarizing societal issues (the United Nations, fluoride, abortion, gay rights, needle distribution programs) is vituperative, violent, and viscious. The reponses create vast chasms that infect attitudes toward much more ordinary matters.

At the moment, those attitude are influenced by a hodgepodge of mechanisms. Principal among them are elements of the media—trendy magazines, syndicated columnists and the editors of feature sections of newspapers, the producers of various entertainment and interview programs seen on television, and movie writers and directors who select the themes and angles of so many socially relevant subjects. In addition, civil behavior is also determined by buyers anxious to get the public to accept new trends in style and new fads, professional commentators in various fields who often feed their views back to the public via the media, and most of all celebrities in sports and entertainment who by virtue of their dress, language, political views, associations, travel patterns, and work ethic influence how the rest of us think about the same topics.^

Civility will improve in our society when some *rationality* is injected into what is considered acceptable behavior and the main impetus for setting trends is wrenched away from the quirky and confusing dominance of the intelligentsia/celebrity/entertainment/professional athlete crowd. We propose that a new mechanism—**Civility Forums**—be created to suggest the norms of civil behavior.

As we see them at this time, any community of any size could form a Civility Forum for itself—a small association of individuals who would be asked to *recommend* the standards and *suggest* appropriate behavior for that group of people. Whatever was recommended or suggested would not be legally enforceable, of course, but should have a chance at general acceptability by virtue of the consideration given to the issues and the compromises forged around the reaction to them.

Some people, almost certainly, will have a knee-jerk aversion to the idea of attempting to "legislate" behavior. But please note that I am not advocating any type of parliamentary process, any form of sin police, or any version of religious courts. These latter two tend to be authoritarian in their interpretations of what is right and wrong, draconian in their enforcement procedures, and generally abhorrent to most in Western societies.

Even though some commentators will surely refer to Civility Forums introduced here as America's version of morality courts, they would not be. For one thing they will not set legally binding rules or operate under some judicial fiat. Civility Forums are seen as *advisory* to the general public and empowered only by the *moral authority* of their recommendations. The day before a Nobel Prize is announced, the winning scientists are generally unknown; after the award, the media transform these same individuals into sages whose opinions on a variety of topics unrelated to their fields is worth seeking and following.^

To understand how we see the purpose of this mechanism for society, we offer a draft of a proposed Founding Resolution that might be adopted by communities.

FOUNDING RESOLUTION

Whereas civility in the community evolves in the course of countless numbers of events and interactions occurring each day;

Whereas acts of kindness or periods of fear continually impact our attitudes toward every one around us;

Whereas the community needs to encourage more acts of kindness, neutralize more examples of discourtesy, and create ways to isolate the activities of those who persist in acts of incivility;

***So therefore be it resolved that** a Civility Forum be formed in this community for the purpose of discussing, debating, and deciding on recommendations for the boundaries of acceptable behavior and suggestions for standards of expectation for interpersonal conduct in our area.*

As we see it, the Founding Resolution provides an institutionalized means where citizens can help form solid, clear, and unambiguous guidance on what the majority of citizens in an area find acceptable *public* behavior.

Here is how the Civility Forums might operate.

1. To have both sufficient public status and some funding, we would encourage the creation of a Center of Cultural Coordination in the Office of the President of the United States. This center could be established through an Executive Order rather than legislation and could be charged with providing a central administrative organization and grant funding authority to assist local and regional Civility Forums to form and operate.

2. Any barrio, neighborhood, zone, urban district, entire city, or metropolitan area could form one or more Civility Forums. Their job would be to meet on occasion or when some convening authority—a home owner's association, neighbor-

hood watch, city council, or county board—identified problems of public behavior and/or asked them to suggest solutions for local problems.

3. Their findings and recommendations would then be funneled to a Regional Civility Forum. To establish the boundaries of these regions, we would divide the country into zones of cultural influence, perhaps 8 to 12 areas that have historical imperatives or share common attitudes on many social issues. Perhaps the best market indicator (as opposed to political guide) for establishing the boundaries of these regions is to match the circulation patterns of major metropolitan newspapers. Where the paper circulates can indicate how thinking on social topics is influenced. But remember that setting these boundaries is not a science and making too much of what areas are in what zones—or where the dividing line of influence between one city paper and another should be drawn—will not be crucial to how the Civility Forums operate. In short, the boundaries won't be perfect, but as a wise person once observed to me: "Perfect should never be a barrier to prevent the possible."^

4. As I see it, each Regional Civility Forum would consist of seven members. Depending on the area itself, the seven participants could be selected by a political body on its own or after the nominations of existing organizations of ministers, educators, athletic managers, police officials, legal

specialists, senior citizens, and youth groups. If existing central organizations or conferences did not want the responsibility of designating a delegate to the Regional Civility Forum, then the federal Center of Cultural Coordination in conjunction with a local political group could call representatives of these groups to a special plenary meeting to select the participants in each Regional Civility Forum.

5. We would hope that each Regional Civility Forum would have a small paid staff that would be responsible for organizing the physical meetings, coordinating the local Civility Forums, and organizing the systematic gathering of local examples of civil and uncivil behavior from television, the Internet, movies, books, recordings, theater, concerts, schools, churches, as well as examples identified by citizens, parents, teachers, coaches, counselors, and ministers. The purpose of these examples would be to determine if some behavior were potentially "bad" or "good" for the community and what kinds of laws, rules, or attitudes might be contributing to those ends. As soon as something approaching a critical mass of these examples was reached (as determined by the "noise level" generated or the number of instances recorded), an *issue* would be identified.^

6. Each of the Regional Civility Forums would then debate the issue around a *Finding*—a simple statement encouraging a particular type of positive

action or recommending a specific way to overcome some negative behavior. The purpose of the *Finding* would be to add an important voice to the circumstances that generate a more civil society. We think that most of the problems would remain regional in nature, sparked by economic, ethnic, or geographic causes peculiar to that region. But of course we anticipate some would require national attention.

7. Whenever an issue arose in more than one Regional Civility Forum and provoked different responses, it would become something of national concern. One "observer" chosen from each Regional Civility Forum would then gather from time to time in a selected city near the geographic center of the country to consider the different regional *Findings* for the same or similar problems. We specifically do not believe that the gathering should be in Washington, D.C.;^ we think putting the highest-level Civility Forum in the capital would weaken the differentiation of its responsibilities from those of the national government. The observers would be expected to try to find common ground on the response to the issue that separated the Regional Civility Forums—through internal debate, accepting testimony, independent professional analysis, or by whatever other means they might decide—so as to be able to offer *national guidance* on the issue at hand.

Our intent in recommending Civility Forums is to try to create the broad boundaries for civil behavior that will leave most people feeling comfortable. If a person were to do things outside of these boundaries, we hope that his or her behavior would be the subject of some form of disapproval, of isolation, of rejection by the vast majority of people.

We would also hope that those operating outside of the boundaries of what would become acceptable civil behavior or those pushing the limits of those boundaries could be encouraged to articulate their need to act in this way. If they do, it could help future Civility Forums to consider widening or changing the boundaries to accommodate those who feel trapped or confined in some way by the guidance offered.

What then is the real spirit behind the concept of Civility Forums? After looking at how this culture as well as others tend to deal with societal change—including the way the standards of the British royal family are watched in the U.K.—we think that those models are now inadequate. Take the case of the United States—a society that looks at change as a dividend that comes with freedom and progress. As investigative author Eric Schlosser reports in *Reefer Madness*: "America is deeply neurotic, a nation divided against itself into a surly, whitewashed mainstream and a lusty, angry, deeply denied subconscious." Perhaps that is the reason the instruments for change are now controlled by *ad hoc*, disparate, and differentially motivated individuals operating on different psychological frequencies.

Sports and entertainment celebrities, for example, are perhaps not entirely conscious of the role they play in effecting social change. Nevertheless, they, have influenced language, dress, attitudes, style, and political beliefs for at least the past 40 years in a far more significant way than their numbers would indicate. We think that the other traditional influential forces in the United States—government, religion, "economic establishment"—were weakened as the country dealt with the shocks to its social fabric. (See pp. 9-10.) In the vacuum, we think people began turning to celebrities for cultural guidance, and what *they* did became the model for the behavior of the rest of the country.

The problem with the celebrity model, from our perspective, is that change for them is a way of getting noticed, a way of advancing a career, making money, increasing their fame, or asserting their power *within* the sphere of the sports/entertainment/leisure industry. Change for them is not necessarily the result of some rational decision or something supported by other developments. Take one of the hottest trends in U.S. television—inexpensive but potentially high-profit reality programming. The genre introduces audiences to real-life people, then follows them through artificial happenings that "traffic in humiliation," and increases "the tension with a series of melodramatic contrivances." Now movies are attempting to duplicate the appeal of filming unscripted encounters, something *The New York Times* thought might not be "a welcome leap forward in entertainment, but ... further evidence of the decay of civilized society."^

For these and other reasons, I believe we deserve something better in deciding societal behavior than copying what appears on television and in movies or mimics the attitudes of famous people without surnames. Should an Elvis, Madonna, Eminem, J. Lo, or Cher dictate how we behave and what we should do?^ Does replicating any of the activities of a Julia Roberts, Britney Spears, David Beckham, Dennis Rodman, John Daly, or any of dozens of other celebrities serve us?^^ I believe our society ought to anchor its standards on something other than the PR marketplace or on what some executive thinks his company can earn by associating with these same people or replicating their individual behavior.

Other societies have faced the idea of structuring behavioral change. But, in my view, they haven't done much better than relying on the random ideas and decisions of the celebrity crowd. Countries like Japan and Britain tend to follow royalty doings with slavish attention, yet they still suffer from some of the same problems found in the United States. Consider also what the fascist governments in Western Europe did in the 1930s, the communist regimes of Eastern Europe tried in the 1950s and 1960s, the Taliban fanatics accomplished in Afghanistan in the 1990s, and the morality police in Saudi Arabia continue to do today. Their results all auger support for the idea that the world needs a new model for establishing social norms.

Our central point is that political conformism of the past as well as the celebrity-driven change mechanism of the West and the religion-driven procedures of the East all fail. America is constantly roiled and affronted by new behaviors; Muslim societies are sapped of energy and initiative in insisting on a rigidity of behavior whether wearing a chador or prohibiting male doctors from treating female patients. Both offer restrictive solutions to difficult problems.

By contrast, the Civility Forums suggested here try to institutionalize a way to deal with change so it isn't disruptive, frightening, or inefficient in its results. Is it worth discussing? Absolutely. Will some dismiss it out of hand with slogans, perjoratives, and unfounded fears? Inevitably. Would it surprise us if the NIH (not invented here) syndrome became a factor in the debate involving various American elites? Of course not.

Does all of this mean that in a quest to make a more civil society we should fail to look for new solutions or fail to experiment with new mechanisms? I hope not. Every country changes. It is how a country deals with that change that makes the difference. When change occurs rapidly and without any form of control, it can be disorienting. As anecdotal proof of this, I offer the following EMail message I received during the winter of 2003 from countless people who got it from an unknown originating source:

> *You know the world is going crazy when the best rapper is a white guy, the best golfer is a black guy, France is accusing the U.S. of arrogance, and Germany doesn't want to go to war.*

124

CONCLUSION

CONCLUSION

We began working on this title in 1997 when we first became aware of the damage corruption outside of the political arena was doing to society. We have been taking notes on what we have observed ever since. Based on those observations, here are the six basic rules for civil behavior.

1. *Be sure of the facts.* Incivility often occurs when people proceed on the basis of false assumptions, process incorrect facts, or develop incomplete evidence.

2. *Exercise patience.* Be sure your facts are right and your understanding is clear before you act against the interests of any other person.

3. *Give other persons the benefit of the doubt.* Don't assume they are being mean or impolite or obtrusive or committing any of a hundred other sins. Assume they forgot, made a mistake, didn't see,

weren't paying attention. In short, give other people the benefit of the doubt whenever possible.

4. *Validate feelings, debate opinions, review theories, but don't argue facts.* If you can't readily prove your assertions of the relevant facts in any discussion, accept the other person's interpretation and move on.

5. *Always ask for forgiveness rather than permission.* This rule should be applied whenever you have to do something that might strike someone else as an act of incivility.

6. *Communicate.* Explain why you are doing what you are doing. Just as a doctor describes each procedure and its probable effect before initiating an injection, inserting a tube, or making an incision, so too anyone involved in public policy should explain what he is about to do before he does it. This has a marvelous way of easing tension and improving trust.

We have also come to realize that repeating slogans such as

- Good ethics are good business—

- Cheaters never prosper—

- Crime doesn't pay—

don't necessarily work to create a more civil society. As Michael Josephson of the Josephson Institute notes: "The problem with promoting ethics in this way is that these assertions about the practical advantages of virtue greatly overstate the case. Unethical conduct frequently [does] work—dishonest citizens pay less taxes, cheaters get good grades, and résumé liars get coveted jobs. Indeed, the prevalence of lying, cheating, and promise-breaking by a lot of smart people suggests that the benefits of high ethical standards are neither certain enough nor substantial enough to deter misconduct."

So why be good? Josephson points out that people who consistently struggle to be good and decent, despite the costs, invariably have better relationships with friends and family and live more rewarding and fulfilling lives. He sees the cost of being good as an investment: "When you do the right thing even when it's personally disadvantageous, you earn the priceless assets of trust, credibility, self-respect, and the affection and esteem of others." Those are the denominations of the basic currency that a civil society needs to exchange.

Now for some final thoughts. While the importance of government in providing the structure for civilization was stated at the outset, government is not a prerequisite for civil behavior. Take the case of Iraq. It emerged in April 2003 from 30 years of totalitarian rule after the United States, the United Kingdom, and Australia invaded to remove Saddam Hussein's regime from power and eliminate any banned weapons uncovered. The British initially installed a sheikh as the new governor of Basra. But as *The Wall Street Journal* reported: "Being governor and being in charge … were two different things … as coalition forces, indigenous Iraqis, exile groups and neighboring countries jockeyed to fill the power vacuum." Government, in short, can only do so much in bringing about civil behavior; people interacting with each other make the ultimate decision on whether a society will enjoy the benefits that civilization offers.

Iraq demonstrated another truism seen in other dictatorships. They are not always as hated as some who live in democracies would assume. Order, stability, tranquility, and peace—the values of civilized behavior—are often more important to some and can be more easily provided by dictatorships than democracies. Take the status of women in post-Baathist Iraq. Under the regime of Saddam Hussein—modeled in many ways after the Soviet Union of Joseph Stalin's time—women "enjoyed a degree of personal liberty" unheard of in other Muslim countries. They attended universities, drove cars, inherited property, filled professional positions, married anyone they liked, and dressed as they pleased. But would the future be better or would these liberties be curtailed by a conservative Shiite-dominated democratic government modeled on their Iranian neighbors?^

We were also recently reminded that civil behavior is very much a two-sided coin in the same way that successful mountain climbers not only worry about how to reach the summit but also how to get back to their base camp as well.^^ In connecting with others in society, you have to know how to act in a civil way *toward* them to attract civil behavior *from* them. What happens to civility, then, when the interaction between groups in a society is not direct but occurs indirectly by example or through role models? Movies are a case in point. We recently saw a little comedy at home with friends called *Big Trouble*, a film about the interactions of several dysfunctional families and groups. The situations were funny and the actors were accomplished, but the writers insisted on adding a stream of foul language and sexual innuendos to nearly every scene. When we checked the label on the DVD jewel case, we were stunned to learn that the kind of language we heard and the allusions we saw are today considered only *potentially* "inappropriate for children under the age of 13."

After watching the film, we questioned why that kind of dialogue was included in any case. What did it add to the film's appeal? It seemed to us—all of whom were beyond retirement age—that the movie would have been just as funny and even more enjoyable without all the swear words and foul insults. We concluded that the producers wanted the language and situations to titillate Hollywood's most coveted audience—14- to 17-year-old boys. Public expressions of otherwise suppressed matters can stimulate talk about the film.^ Nevertheless, our friends said that the dialog is a sign of the deterioration of civility in our society, that it promotes disrespect and bad behavior in public. My wife agreed.

I said that I doubted their conclusion. I argued from the position of situational behavior. I pointed out that behavior is not an absolute set of actions and reactions but activity that is adjusted to the place and condition an individual finds.^^ In the case at hand, the bad language was not used in a restaurant or park—where it would be clearly inappropriate by all current standards—but part of a make-believe story that was neither realistic nor plausible. It was, in short, just a movie. Like violent videos and other fantasies, the vast majority of viewers do not take on-screen actions as license for off-screen activities. While some studies have shown that a tiny percentage of the population cannot properly separate what is watched on television, acted out in videos, or seen in the movies, nearly everyone else knows what is acceptable real-life behavior and what is not.

What to do then about the small percentage who tend to emulate and/or duplicate what they see? I believe it remains the role of parents, teachers, counselors, ministers, doctors, coaches, and grandparents to make sure that all kids they come in contact with understand that real life should not be confused with fantasy situations and that there is a difference between acceptable civil behavior and the incivility that causes so much damage to society.

My wife and I took our then going on three-year-old granddaughter to a performance of the *Snow Queen* at the Falcon Theatre. Everything about the performance was splendid, and little Maya sat stone still in the second row with eyes wide throughout the entire performance. She had a memorable time, as did we.

On the way out of the theater we noticed a sign. It asked the audience to be respectful of the theater's residential neighbors, to keep conversations soft, to watch the volume of car radios, to drive slowly and carefully out of the area. Nice touch. It was a reminder to patrons that while the theater is located on a major commercial street, it backs up onto a neighborhood of nice homes where people deserve to enjoy all aspects of their lives in peace as well. We don't know how many violations of the informal code occur in a year—and we suspect some backsliding as old habits come into play or memories lapse—but we suspect that this request for civility is honored. The point is that we often have to remind people to be civil. If we do, for the most part they are.

Another situation occurred to the two of us, but this time we did not have our granddaughter in tow. We went to a new Japanese restaurant the other day close to our home. We were early but not the first. Another couple was seated in a booth near the front entrance. We noticed that the man was in a coat and tie, which is unusual in this day and age, but since I too was coming from the office, I was dressed the same way.

We took a booth some distance away. As we were reviewing the menu, we heard a torrent of loud conversation. Without looking, it was clear the man was speaking on a cell phone. As the one-sided conversation picked up in volume and speed, you knew that the guy was getting more and more agitated. It was not long before my wife was looking at me and I was paying attention to the conversation. It was clear that the man was yelling at his housekeeper, who apparently was reporting on some transgression committed by a paid contractor or workman. The man in the coat and tie was obviously mad at what the contractor had done and was directing his anger at the housekeeper.

The housekeeper must have objected to the abuse, because the guy became even more infuriated and a torrent of F-words and expletives poured forth. My wife said she wanted to leave; I said I would take care of it. I marched to the man's table and stood over him, staring. He looked at me puzzled, then told the person at the other end to hold on. I said in an even voice that I thought his language was inappropriate, that my wife had become uncomfortable, that we deserved to enjoy our peace as much as he would want to enjoy his, that it was not acceptable language in public, that if he wanted to have that kind of conversation he needed to go to his car or the Men's room or somewhere else where others didn't have to put up with it.

He was obviously stunned by the approach and the fluidity of the complaint I was lodging, but to his credit he did absolutely the civil thing. He immediately apologized, nodded that he understood my distress, and as I was leaving to return to my table, his conversation on the phone had dropped to a whisper and it seemed to be more logical and less emotional. A few minutes later, the man came to our table and apologized again, this time to my wife. He said he was very sorry that he had disturbed our meal and that he had not respected our right to privacy. When they left the restaurant, he again waved to say once again that he had gotten our message and would make amends.

Both my wife and I thought that it was a classy way to respond to a complaint. Rather than get angry for an interfering in his business, he clearly saw the problem from our perspective.

It was another way of living the Golden Rule. If we all did that, we would have less anger, fewer problems, and more civility.

Finally, if respect and trust are the two ingredients that define civility, then suspicion and/or discovery of hypocrisy must be what provokes incivility.^ Take the situation in Baghdad as U.S. troops continued to investigate the palaces of Saddam Hussein and those favored by his regime. These people had denounced the United States as infidels and sinners, but they loved what it produced to support their lifestyle. As a reporter for the *Los Angeles Times* noted:

> *For all of its claims to Islamic piety, the regime's elite was Western to the core. Their grand homes hid American computers, whisky, pornography, videos and pop music. They drove big Chevys, smoked Marlboros and read Newsweek.*

Civilization depends on honesty, trust, and respect. The Iraqi regime lacked it, and the rest of the world recognized that fact. But the rest of the world also needs to look at structures in their own countries to determine how well honesty, trust, and respect are flourishing in their own societies. When they do, all of us will be better off.

APPENDIX

ACKNOWLEDGMENTS

I began working on this book at the time I finished *Grandparenting* and as I started writing *Corruption.* The three books have been less than a year in the making primarily because of a writing methodology I adopted some years ago. My habit has been to make notes whenever a thought occurs to me, record what I hear whenever a point sounds important to me, and cut out an article or underline a phrase whenever I read something that seems relevant to me. Then when I feel I have a sufficient grasp of a topic in my head, I need only assemble the notes and papers in my file into a coherent whole. As a result, all those who have made comments to me, engaged me in conversation, sent me an EMail, passed along something to read, or asked me for my views have had a hand in the development of these books. I can't remember the precise circumstances of each contribution and I can't name the individuals who made them, but if you read a reference to a discussion we had, see something you sent to me, or come across an idea you expressed to me, my profound thanks for what you have given me.

Others have provided more easily identifiable help and deserve a more personal note of appreciation: Mustafa Akyol of Istanbul for translating and interpreting the Muslim version of the Golden Rule; Bill Butler, who gave me a booklet he acquired on a visit to Cairo that added so much to my thinking on civility and religion; my wife, Barbara DeKovner-Mayer, who related many of the family examples I have used and reviewed the manuscript for me; Zan Green, who sent me his ideas on the dangers of left-handed cell phone users; Arnika Gumbiner, whose comments on contemporary events so often sparked my own sometimes contrary responses; my son, Kennith Harris, who taught me about situational behavior and reminds me of the important difference between facts and feelings; my Mother, Victoria Harris, who continues to provide understanding and support for all of my writing efforts; Douglas Lister of London who shared some of his mobile phone experiences with me; Lorraine Rothman for assisting me in identifying appropriate biblical quotations; and Richard Sherer for so willingly providing a personal word-finder source of unparalleled accuracy and quickness.

Special appreciation also again go to my dedicated corps of readers—Bill Gumbiner, David Harris, Michael Harris, and Adolf Shvedchikov—who reviewed a draft of this book to give me their comments and changes. So, too, to my editor, Charles (Chuck) Goldman, a gentle, understanding, and enormously talented individual. Like all great editors, he is much more than a walking thesaurus or a living style manual. He is willing to look at issues of grammar and syntax in ways that advance the language in writing as it marches ahead orally. As always, though, none of these people should be blamed for what you have read. That is my ultimate responsibility, and your complaints should be directed to me rather than to them.

One more group deserves special attention—the attentive talent behind the scenes: Bill Floyd at Fidlar Doubleday, who does our pre-press work; Diane Tupper Sieck of International Artwork, who provides the bar codes and a lot more; John Osborne of Night Shift Graphics in England, who creates our covers; and Penelope Morensen and Desiree Vidal of the staff of The Americas Group. Our thanks also to distributors such as Luigi Rizzo and Dawood Salabbai who keep our books flowing to the marketplace, and to Steve Dawson, Kelly Galusha, and Tom Sims of Overseas Book Services for providing us with the mechanism to give our ideas international exposure at various book fairs.

CIVILITY

BIBLIOGRAPHIC NOTES

The page numbers in the left-hand column identify the place where a reference or the first words of a quotation can be found in the text of the book.

15   "Do unto others"—Matthew 7:12.

16   "What is hateful" and "This is the"—Taken from a 1992 guide book for visitors to Ben Ezra Synagogue in Cairo.

17   "what began...as" and "guns are as"—*The New York Times,* March 27, 2003. "Maybe if there"—*The New York Times,* April 1, 2003.

18   The contentious issue between Muslims and Hindus has been dormant for nearly three years. Now, a broken pillar with a lotus flower carving was uncovered at the site, suggesting "there exists a permanent structure beneath the soil."—*Arizona Republic,* April 2, 2003.
      "Voluntary association[s], a"—from an article by Shlomo Avineri, professor of Political Science at The Hebrew University, reprinted in the *Los Angeles Times*, April 13, 2003.

19   The issue of manners in public reminded us of a classic comment by Israel's Shimon Peres. When asked about a public opinion poll that showed how popular he remained among elements of Israel's Labor Party, he said: "Polls are like perfume. Nice to smell, dangerous to swallow." (*Los Angeles Times*, January 24, 2003.) So it is with bad manners. A temporary gain resulting from some act of discourtesy can nevertheless lead to long-term regrets.

20   See Godfrey Harris, *Corruption,* The Americas Group, 2003.

21   *The Wall Street Journal* notes that when a floor trader complained that he couldn't get a specialist to execute his order until the price had risen, the chairman of the New York Stock Exchange personally called to apologize. More than any other stock market, the New York Stock Exchange runs on trust "because it's the last major exchange that relies upon human traders [to set prices] on a central, physical floor." (April 18, 2003.)

22   "The softess pillow"—Taken from an advertisement seen on CBS television on March 30, 2003.

23   "[T]he war [in...]" —*The New York Times,* March 28, 2003.

24   "These days it"—*Los Angeles Times*, April 20, 2003.
      "must provide visual"— *The New York Times*, March 27, 2003.

25   Bob Woodward describes debates between Vice President Dick Cheney and Secretary of State Colin Powell as "dancing on the edge of civility but not departing from the formal propriety that [they] generally showed each other." Bob Woodward, *Bush at War*, Simon & Schuster, 2002, p. 346.

26   "France said this" and "How many Frenchmen"—Reported on Fox News on February 16, 2003.

28   Often reconciliation is needed between the more powerful few and the less powerful many. Take darts. According to the (London) *Sunday Mirror* for March 16, 2003, the game may soon be subjected to a range of local regulations that can declare the play of darts either "too dangerous"—thus requiring pub owners to install expensive enclosures for play—or "too entertaining"—thus requiring pub owners to pay for an additional license. Other pubs have other problems involving civility. Those playing music that results in dancing are also being told that they, too, need entertainment licenses. The

purpose is to insure adequate noise control. But the issue of what actually constitutes dancing is now engaging bureaucrats, lawyers, pub management, and patrons. See *The New York Times,* April 29, 2003.

29   "Anything that comes" and "very, very bizarre"—*The* (Sunday) *Telegraph,* March 16, 2003.

^   In the U.S., the textbook publishers are now sanitizing material beyond "derogatory racist and sexist bias" to past common sense. In *The Language Police,* Diane Ravitch, documents how jargon-filled, controversy-adverse, textbooks forbid such things as mention of the elderly as poor, infirm or lonely lest "ageism" be fostered. Ravitch urges forbidden terms and words to be exposed to public light where ridicule may end the hijacking of education by special interests. Editorial, *Los Angeles Times,* May 4, 2003.

30   "an essentially American"—Tim Katz, *Los Angeles Times,* March 30, 2003.

32   Here is how a question of civility was recently handled in South Korea. When a newly elected reformist legislator arrived to be sworn in wearing beige slacks and a T-shirt under a Navy blue jacket, several members walked out in protest, others criticized him "for defaming the Assembly." Once in suit and tie(!), he was allowed to take his seat. *The New York Times,* May 1, 2003.
      "both mental and"—*Los Angeles Times,* April 20, 2003.

35   It should be noted that SARS is just one of a number of new and deadly infections that have emerged in the last few decades since the eradication of smallpox and the effective control of malaria. *The New York Times* reports that "since 1973, about 30 new pathogens, including Ebola and HIV, have appeared." —*The New York Times,* April 1, 2003.

36   *The Wall Street Journal* for April 16, 2003, notes that it took more than two years for another mysterious virus—HIV—to be isolated and "several more to unravel its genes. Fast forward to 2003. Just two months after the first inklings of another deadly diseased emerged ... scientists have not only identified the culprit but fully decoded its genetic makeup. [T]his coup is a case study in modern science at warp speed ... us[ing] Internet links and a high-tech new scientific detective kit—a sliver of silicon containing bits of genetic material from all 1000 known viruses" to identify the virus.
      "SARS is caused"—*ibid.*

37   "struck them even"— *The New York Times,* April 17, 2003.
      "could drain $10.6 ..." —*The Wall Street Journal,* April 21, 2003.

^   As the *Los Angeles Times* (May 3, 2003) noted, SARS has infected many thousands while "severe acute fear syndrome (SAFS) has infected millions" because of "TV's unspoken urgency and unwarrntged visual credibility."

38   "I don't think"—*Los Angeles Times,* April 6, 2003.
      "unprecedented" and "the virus has"—*Los Angeles Times,* April 27, 2003.

41   See David Behar, Godfrey Harris, and Ross W. Simpson, *Invasion: The American Destruction of the Noriega Regime in Panama,* The Americas Group, 1990, pp. 76–80, and Guillermo de St. Malo A. and Godfrey Harris, *The Panamanian Problem: How the Reagan and Bush Administrations Dealt with the Noriega Regime,* The Americas Group, 1993, pp. 263–264.

44   "Most people watching"—Michael Crichton, *Prey,* Harper Collins, 2002, p. 125–126.

139

46   For the record, *The Essential Event Planning Kit* is described as a step-by-step system to help organize and manage any meeting, dinner, visit, wedding, exhibit, reception, or party—on time, within budget, and without stress—by using 11 freely reproducible forms and simple instructions. The Americas Group, 2003.

48   For a revealing look at tort lawyers and their motivations. see John Grisham's novel *King of Torts,* 2003.

49   Juries are not the only culprits in the legal system. Listen to a letter written to the *(*London) *Telegraph* on March 15, 2003: "Idiot judges who excuse the behaviour of persistent offenders ... [corrode] society. We are now called irresponsible if we don't make our homes like Fort Knox. The onus on us is to prevent crime and criminals are regarded as the victims of society."

51   Rick Reilly, in his weekly column in *Sports Illustrated* (April 28, 2003) writes: "[T]he next time some genius with more beer in him than brains decides to run onto the field ..., baseball needs to do nothing at all. For five minutes, I want security to move with the speed of postal clerks with bunions. Because for those five minutes players from both teams will be piled on top of Tommy Twelvepack, reconfiguring the joker into steak tartar."
"two, unencumbered by"—*Sports Illustrated,* January 27, 2003.

52   "The plane from"—*Ibid.*

53   "Always know where" and other quotes all from Hertz, *Safety Tips,* 2000.

55   "The premise of" and "of rude indifference" from Sue Fox, *Etiquette for Dummies,* quoted in *Los Angeles Times,* March 30, 2003. Judith Martin (Ms. Manners) sees American etiquette as a means of demonstrating equality rather than obsequiousness. Both George Washington and Thomas Jefferson were "convinced that European etiquette was outmoded. [But] how do you treat people as equals and still have respect?"—See *Time,* December 2, 2002. For another interesting take on manners, see Lamont K. Roberts. *Kiss That Neanderthal Good-Bye,* Channel Point Media Group, 2001.

^   Basic table manners have all but disappeared "with the advent of [a] hurried lifestyle, ... takeout convenience. Social events, too, have become more casual, with food stations ...as popular as served meals."—Fox, *op. cit.*

60   "Couples doing their" and all other quotations from (London) *Telegraph Magazine,* March 15, 2003.

67   The concept of how you say something now concerns the editors of the *New Oxford American Dictionary. The Wall Street Journal* (May 1, 2003) reports that the editors are discussing adding a definition to the next edition for the entry "shut up"—now explained as a command for silence. The words have ameliorated (in linguistic terms) to express "disbelief, shock, and joy"—as in "Oh my God" or "No way"—but only when they are spoken with a full stop between the two words and a rising inflection on the word "up." Without the special rhythm, the phrase "can sound too much like an affront." See also Godfrey Harris, *Watch It!,* The Americas Group, 2001.

73   "To thine own" —William Shakespeare, *Hamlet,* Act I Scene 3.

74   "On Thursday, March"—*The Wall Street Journal,* April 4, 2003.

75   "Eligibility for execution" and "To execute a" taken from the *Miami Herald,* February 11, 2003.

81   A case in point on waiting. *The New York Times* recently changed its deliv-
      ery service. A paper that had been delivered to us by 4:00 in the morning was
      now turning up at 8:30. One day when it hadn't shown up by 9:00, I called to
      give the operator and the monitoring equipment an earful of invective until I
      was sweetly interrupted with the news that it was a transmission/production
      problem, not a delivery issue. It reminded me how hard it is sometimes to
      remember my own lessons on civil behavior. Get all the facts first!

83   "the importance of"—Godfrey Harris and Kennith L Harris, *Concentration,*
      Second Edition, The Americas Group, 2000, p. i.

85   One of our other books does. See Godfrey Harris, *Talk Is Easy—How to
      Make Every Conversation Pay Off,* The Americas Group, 1999.

102   "has the ability"—Quoted in *Los Angeles Times,* May 3, 2003.
      "Put golf in"—First Tee advertisement seen on CBS television during the
      2003 Masters Golf Tournament, April 12–13, 2003.

115   Not all new trends in civil behavior come from prominent and/or notorious
      sources. Take the matter of "slugging"—that peculiar blend of hitchhiking
      and carpooling that has arisen in Northern Virginia where solo drivers pick
      up total strangers to be able to drive "to work in high-occupancy-vehicle
      lanes." The practice greatly reduces commuting time, highway traffic, and
      parking problems. It has operated without incident or government regula-
      tion. It has also developed its own etiquette of speaking, cell phone use,
      boarding, and more. *The New York Times,* April 29, 2003.

116   See Baruch A. Shalev, *100 Years of Nobel Prizes*—Second Edition, The
      Americas Group, 2002.

118   Condoleeza Rice used different words to describe the same thought in a
      statement to the National Security Council: "Make sure the best is not the
      enemy of the good." Bob Woodward, *Bush at War,* Simon & Schuster, 2002,
      p. 112.

119   Appropriate dress is one such issue in almost continuous play. We hold that
      dressing in coat and tie honors the participants by proclaiming that the event
      is *special*; others justify wearing informal clothing as more comfortable. We
      say that civility is about appreciating all that society offers everyone, not
      about what may feel good for a single individual at any given moment.

120   For precedence, note that other offices with national stature—even govern-
      ment offices—are not located in Washington, D.C., from the Centers for
      Disease Control and Prevention (Atlanta) to the Social Security Administra-
      tion (Baltimore).

121   "America is deeply"—Quoted in *Time,* April 28, 2003.

122   "traffic in humiliation"— *The New York Times,* April 24, 2003.
      "the tension with" and "a welcome leap"—*The New York Times*, April 21,
      2003.

^   Despite the near-universal critical condemnation of the reality genre, you
      have to admire the *chutzpah* of the producers of *The Real Cancun*. In their
      newspaper ads promoting the film, they cheerfully use the good and bad
      from a review by Scot Foundas of *Daily Variety:* "Unabashedly tasteless,
      wholly trashy—and hugely entertaining." Nevertheless, box office ticket sales
      are said to have proven to be disappointing.

123   It seems that one of America's celebrity-focused magazines, the *Star,* reports only on those known by their first names and nicknames, a group of personalities particularly popular with younger audiences.

^^   Although no professional American football players are named in our list of personalities, so many players end up on the wrong side of the law that agent Leigh Steinberg says: "NFL teams are using services that are checking on every arrest, checking for substance abuse, asking questions on campus, talking to anyone and everyone."—*Los Angeles Times,* April 20, 2003.

127   "The problem with"—Michael Josephson, "Character Counts" segment heard on KNX radio in Los Angeles on January 30, 2003.

128   "When you do"—*Ibid.*

        "Being governor and"—*The Wall Street Journal,* April 11, 2003.

129   "enjoyed a degree" —*Los Angeles Times,* April 27, 2003.

^   For a comprehensive discussion of American-style democracy abroad, see Guillermo de St. Malo A. and Godfrey Harris, *The Panamanian Problem: How the Reagan and Bush Administrations Dealt with the Noriega Regime,* The Americas Group, 1993, pp. 104–110.

^^   No where were the two sides of the same topic more clearly expressed than in articles commenting on the 50th anniversary of the climbing of Mount Everest by Sir Edmund Hillary and Tenzing Norgay. When Hillary was asked to comment on whether English school teacher George Mallory's 1924 attempt to reach the summit had been successful—Mallory's mummified body had been found on an approach slope in 1999—Hillary said: "Getting to the bottom is an important part, too." (*Sports Illustrated,* April 14, 2003.)

130   "inappropriate for children" and "strongly"—from the rating system of the Motion Picture Association of America. Their privately developed, privately maintained system has been accepted by the public as authoritative.

^   For a detailed discussion of word of mouth advertising, see Godfrey Harris, *Don't Take Our Word For It,* The Americas Group, 1998.

^^   As noted above, situational behavior is no more apparent than in the clothes we choose to wear. A funny moment in the English 2002 film *Bend It Like Beckham* is a case in point. The mother of a girl soccer player agrees to see her daughter play. When the mother finally climbs into the family car for the ride to the grounds, she is wearing a flowery frock and broad brimmed hat. Her husband looks at her and says: "You're going to a football match, not bloody Ascot." See also Godfrey Harris, *Grandparenting,* The Americas Group, 2002, pp. 30–36. Another comment on dress appears at p. 119 above.

134   While hypocrisy shatters the bonds of civility, humiliation poisons the opportunities for reconciliation of peoples with disparate beliefs. Take the Iraq War. Arab civil behavior is said to be based on "three pillars: courage-bravery, hospitality-generosity, and honor-dignity." Yet the collapse of the defenses of Baghdad cast doubt on the Arab concept of bravery; the failure to forge a common Arab position before the war affected the idea of brotherhood; and the U.S. defeat of Iraq challenged Arab honor by helping Israel. Quotation in *Los Angeles Times,* April 24, 2003, taken from Raphael Patai's 1973 book, *The Arab Mind.*

INDEX

APPENDIX

CIVILITY

ABOUT THE AUTHOR

GODFREY HARRIS has been a public policy consultant based in Los Angeles, California, since 1968. He began consulting after serving as a university lecturer, a U.S. Army intelligence officer, a U.S. foreign service officer with the Department of State, an organizational specialist in President Lyndon Johnson's Executive Office, and a program manager for an international financial company in Geneva.

As president of Harris/Ragan Management Group, Harris has focused the firm's activities on projects that offer alternative solutions to matters of community concern. In fulfilling that role, he has specialized in political and economic analysis, marketing public and private sector services through word of mouth advertising, developing new environmental and commercial products, creating commemorative events, and promoting international tourism to various destinations.

Harris has taught political science and comparative government at UCLA and Rutgers University; conducted tourism seminars at the University of Hawaii, Clemson University, and for the U.S. Embassy, London; and lectured on marketing for the Tyrol Tourist Authority, the San Diego County Parks and Recreation Department, and the National Energy Management Institute. This is the 38th book he has written on his own or with associates. He holds degrees from Stanford University and the University of California, Los Angeles.